Middlesex County Cricket Club
President: Clive Radley MBE
Life vice-presidents: Don Bennett, Phil Edmonds, Bob Gale, Ron Gerard OBE KStJ, Alan Moss, Mike Murray, Geoff Norris, Peter Parfitt, Charles Robins

Executive Board:
Ian Lovett (chairman), Mike O'Farrell (honorary treasurer), Vinny Codrington (chief executive), Angus Fraser MBE (managing director of cricket), Bob Baxter (chairman of Middlesex Cricket Board), Chris Lowe (elected candidate, until 2016), Paul Downton (elected candidate, until 2016), Simon Shepard (elected candidate, until 2015), Alvan Seth-Smith (elected candidate, until 2015), David Kendix (elected candidate, until 2014), Chris Goldie (elected candidate, until 2014)

Editor: John Stern
Consultant editor: Marcus Williams
Designer: Joe Provis
Printed by Jellyfish Print Solutions
Published by Trinorth Ltd

The editor would like to offer special thanks to: Vinny Codrington, Ian Lovett, Clive Radley, Alvan Seth-Smith, Steve Fletcher, Rebecca Hart, Rupert Jones and all at Middlesex CCC; Clayton Beerman; MCC; William Powell; all contributors and interviewees.

Photography: Matt Bright, Middlesex CCC photo archive, Getty Images, Roger Mann Collection, MCC, Vince van der Bijl, Sarah Williams.

Statistics source: cricketarchive.co.uk

The views and opinions expressed in this brochure are those of the individual contributors and do not necessarily reflect the views of Middlesex County Cricket Club.

Copyright This publication is copyright of Middlesex County Cricket Club. Reproduction in whole or part is strictly prohibited without prior consent of Middlesex CCC.

CONTENTS

150TH ANNIVERSARY

PATRONS

J.H. Cook	S. Harrop
W.F. Frewen	P. Lucas

G.W. Norris

~~~~~

CORPORATE PARTNERS

BROOKS MACDONALD *

SPORTING INDEX
WORLD LEADERS IN SPORTS SPREAD BETTING

VAUXHALL

PLB

RUSTENBERG
WINES

Middlesex Cricket would like to thank
all of our 150th Anniversary
Patrons & Corporate Partners.

"THERE HAS ONLY EVER BEEN ONE TEAM FOR ME"

CLIVE RADLEY, MIDDLESEX CCC PRESIDENT

PRESIDENTS OF MIDDLESEX CCC

1866–98	Viscount Enfield (later the Earl of Stafford)
1899–1906	VE Walker
1907–22	RD Walker
1923–36	AJ Webbe
1937–46	Sir Pelham Warner
1947–49	FT Mann
1950–57	RH Twining
1958–62	GEV Crutchley
1963–76	GC Newman
1977–79	GOB Allen
1980–82	WH Webster
1983–90	FG Mann
1991–97	DCS Compton
1997–99	MP Murray
1999–2001	R Gerard
2001–03	RA Gale
2003–05	AE Moss
2005–07	RVC Robins
2007–09	D Bennett
2009–11	PH Parfitt
2011–13	GW Norris
2013–	CT Radley

I first arrived at Lord's in 1961 as a 17-year-old and have been here ever since. I was brought up in Norfolk and played for them briefly when Bill Edrich was captain. He recommended to Middlesex that they offer me a three-year contract without even having a trial. After the first couple of weeks I think they thought that old Bill had made a bit of a mistake but more than 50 years later I'm still here. There has only ever been one team for me – I'm Middlesex through and through.

It probably took me six or seven years even to talk to the likes of Fred Titmus or John Murray. One of the first things I said to Fred when he was driving me up north for an away trip was to ask him about my first day at Middlesex. I'd had a net when I first arrived from Norfolk and it was a nightmare. I couldn't lay a bat on it. Alan Moss and Don Bennett were bowling and the ball was nipping back, hitting me on the thigh or passing the outside edge. I could see Titmus and Murray at the end of the net shaking their heads. So all these years later I plucked up the courage to ask Fred what he thought. He said: "We both said to each other that we thought Bill Edrich was a good judge but that he'd got this bloke wrong!"

My first coach was the great Jack Robertson, a lovely man who never said anything – probably because he thought I was such a terrible player. But I think I worked it out enough to make the most of the potential I had which, when I became head coach of MCC, was all I wanted to see from young lads. I was happy as long as they fulfilled their potential, whether they did that with a bit of help from a coach or worked it out for themselves.

There have been some ups and downs along the way but I wouldn't have swapped it for the world. The sides captained by Mike Brearley and Mike Gatting were brilliant teams to be a part of. I didn't realise it at the time but success breeds success and everyone loves to be in a winning side whether you have succeeded personally or not. Within the pages of this terrific brochure you will find all those great times relived by many of the Middlesex legends who made them happen. There are plenty of great stories.

These are exciting times again at Middlesex with impressive results on the field and some very promising young players emerging as well. Our 150th anniversary year promises to be a memorable one on and off the field with a number of superb events planned.

I do hope that all Middlesex followers will join us in supporting these events and help make 2014 a true celebration of this great club.

A LEGACY OF LEADERSHIP

GILES CLARKE, ECB CHAIRMAN

On behalf of the England and Wales Cricket Board, I would like to take this opportunity to send warm congratulations to everyone connected with Middlesex CCC on reaching such a significant milestone in the club's history.

The origins of cricket clearly have some of their roots in the county of Middlesex from at least the 16th century. The huge growth in the game's popularity lay in the founding of our great county clubs and Middlesex's long, proud and illustrious history is inextricably linked with the home of cricket, Lord's, itself.

I believe the club's greatest legacy to the wider game has been its production of great England captains. No fewer than 12 Middlesex players have led England including five Ashes winners: AE Stoddart, 'Plum' Warner, Mike Brearley, Mike Gatting and most recently, of course, Andrew Strauss.

On a personal basis, like many others my literary introduction to the game was through the legendary Middlesex and England captain Sir Pelham Warner's writings and musings. His own long attachment to, and his affection for, the county have been mirrored by Mike Gatting and it is highly appropriate such a Middlesex stalwart should be MCC president in 2014 to celebrate the 150th anniversary.

The club's long record of success in both the County Championship and limited-overs formats has also produced many legendary England players, with Denis Compton and Bill Edrich enshrined in post-war memory, and Patsy Hendren pre-war.

With the club enjoying an excellent season in the LV= County Championship Division One in 2013 and boasting current England players such as Steven Finn and Eoin Morgan in their ranks and a host of promising youngsters, Middlesex supporters can look forward to the future with optimism.

The appointment of the former England fast bowler Angus Fraser as managing director of cricket has proved to be a particularly shrewd move, and in Ian Lovett as chairman and Vinny Codrington as chief executive Middlesex possess two men who bring a wealth of cricketing knowledge and business expertise to the club's off-field administration.

We trust that 2014 proves to be a very memorable year in the club's history and wish you all a very happy 150th birthday.

SO MUCH IN COMMON

DEREK BREWER, MCC CHIEF EXECUTIVE & SECRETARY

Two thousand and fourteen is a momentous year for MCC and Middlesex alike – it marks the bicentenary of the current Lord's Ground as well as the 150th birthday of the county club.

It is a happy coincidence, and one that means both clubs should really be able to make the most of their respective celebrations, one example of which will be the President of MCC's XI v President of Middlesex's XI match at Lord's. Entirely appropriately, MCC's President, who will oversee this special year, is Mike Gatting – a man inextricably linked with both clubs.

Middlesex is in a unique position among the first-class counties in that it shares its home ground with another club which, of course, means it has to take its cricket elsewhere around the county when fixtures clash. Yet I very much hope everyone related to Middlesex – players, staff and members alike – view Lord's as their home. Certainly the bonds between the two clubs are strong, and with the likes of Mike Brearley, Angus Fraser and Mike Gatting sitting on the MCC Committee, the affection for Middlesex starts right at the very top.

Everyone at MCC wishes Middlesex success on the field. After all, the greater the number of cricket fans inclined to make the trip to St John's Wood, the better for us both. Indeed, Lord's hosted a couple of really electric nights in the Friends Life t20 in July 2013 in front of crowds in excess of 20,000 – a great advert for the most modern format of the game played on the most historic and traditional of stages.

In the coming years MCC is seeking to ensure that stage – Lord's – develops into unquestionably the finest cricket ground in the world. The Club's 15-year Masterplan is aimed at improving facilities for everyone who uses the ground, retaining the size of both the Main and Nursery Grounds, constructing architecturally-significant stands and maintaining the unique character of Lord's with gardens and trees.

I hope Middlesex's finest continue to grace the Home of Cricket as they have done since 1877 and benefit from MCC's development of the ground. I'm sure the celebrations in 2014 will reflect the long and happy relationship the two clubs have shared.

FROM NAÏVE STUDENT TO ENGLAND CAPTAIN

Andrew Strauss on how it all began at Lord's and his hopes for the future

I can remember it like it was yesterday. I was 19 and wide-eyed as I walked, with my bag over my shoulder, through the Grace Gates for my Middlesex trial. It was June 1996, the first team were playing Warwickshire in the County Championship and Shaun Pollock was bowling to Paul Weekes and Jason Pooley.

I headed over to the nets on the Nursery Ground where I pitted myself against the county second-team bowlers, the likes of Jamie Hewitt and Tim Bloomfield. It was quite a nervous moment to put it mildly. I hadn't had anything to do with the Middlesex age-group sides and hadn't played any second-team cricket. I was at Durham University and my old school coach Andy Wagner, who knew Middlesex's second-team coach Ian Gould from back in the day, arranged a trial. It was extraordinary to have the opportunity to play at Lord's and such a massive culture shock from playing club cricket.

It was a massive thrill to play at Lord's, where I had watched my first Test match in 1990. I made runs on my debut in 1998 which proved to me that I could perform at that level but I just didn't know anything about professional cricket at that stage. I'd always just played it as a recreation and suddenly I was in this professional environment. Gould pushed me and Ben Hutton quite hard and made us realise that we were a long way short of where we needed to be.

I was wonderfully naïve in many ways. I loved the game and I loved the idea of being paid to play but I had no idea what that entailed. So it was a steep learning curve. And while Middlesex wasn't a harsh environment exactly it was a typical county dressing room with quite a strong hierarchy. There was lots of banter and mickey-taking, plenty of which seemed to be directed

> **I have always had a great fondness for Middlesex. From the moment I turned up there I got treated really well and it is my club**

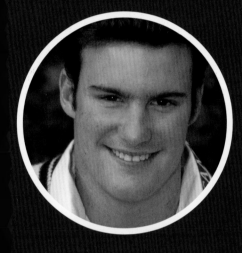

ANDREW JOHN STRAUSS

Born: March 2, 1977, Johannesburg
Left-hand batsman

- 8,591 first-class runs (17,046 overall) for Middlesex at 42.95, 20 hundreds, 1998–2012
- Highest score 241* v Leicestershire 2011
- 7,037 runs in 100 Tests, 21 hundreds
- 2,979 one-day runs for Middlesex, 3 hundreds
- Middlesex cap 2001
- Middlesex captain 2002–04, winning promotion to Division 1 of the County Championship in 2002
- Captained England to Ashes victories in 2009 and 2010-11 and Test No.1 ranking in 2011
- Awarded MBE in 2006 and OBE in 2011
- Wisden Cricketer of the Year 2005
- Middlesex benefit 2009

at me and Ben, being young, naïve public-school idiots.

It was a period of great change at the club. At the start the old guard were still there – Don Bennett was coach and Mike Gatting was captain – but within 12 months it all changed. Don had retired and John Buchanan came in. Mark Ramprakash had taken over the captaincy. We went through quite a long period of instability with a number of changes of coach and captain.

As a young guy trying to establish myself in the team, I didn't get involved in club politics but it was a frustrating time for many people because this was a club used to winning trophies. Suddenly we found ourselves at the bottom of the County Championship and falling a long way short of where we wanted to be. The coaches started to feel the pressure and so the players felt pressurised themselves. No one is completely unaffected by a situation like that.

In 2002 I became captain, pretty much out of the blue. I remember being really shocked that Angus Fraser was retiring. He'd done a really good job with the side and spent a lot of time and effort with the younger players, trying to create a family environment again. We'd lost the likes of Justin Langer and Mark Ramprakash but actually started playing a bit better because the youngsters were revelling in taking more responsibility.

I don't think I was ready to captain a county side but it forced me to grow up quickly and think for the first time about leadership and how to set an example. It was a pretty stressful first six months or so but thankfully I batted well and you earn people's respect through the consistency of your performances.

We got promoted that season which was a big step forward and then we stayed in the first division so we were going in the right direction. It was a really wonderful, fun time to be a Middlesex cricketer. There were a lot of young guys who were all pretty close mates and our families all joined in too.

From the winter of 2003 at least half of my attention was given over to England and it just wasn't tenable for me to captain any more. That was my best season with the bat, a coming of age as a batsman that helped my captaincy.

Spending so much time with England made it hard to maintain a connection with the club though it has been easier since Angus came back into the mix because he's a good friend of mine. In the latter years I think I was viewed as a bit of a sounding board because I was further removed and could be impartial. I quite liked that role. I was always conscious of not turning up to Lord's and giving it 'the big 'un'. I didn't want to step on any toes.

I have always had a great fondness for Middlesex. From the moment I turned up there I got treated really well and it is my club. It is a shame that I didn't play more for Middlesex over the last seven or eight years of my career but I'd like to think when I did come back I gave it my all and got some important runs for the team. I quite like that I finished off with a hundred against Nottinghamshire at Uxbridge though I would have loved to have played in a one-day final or won the County Championship.

I love where the club are at the moment. They've got a really good set-up and some really good young players. Richard Scott and Angus have done a fantastic job and it's a real pleasure for me to see some stability in the club again.

Everyone involved with Middlesex is really pleased to see them back near the top of the County Championship and competing again in Twenty20 and one-day cricket. It feels like a return to winning trophies is not that far away now. ●

THE MIDDLESEX WAY

Managing director of cricket **Angus Fraser** looks back on his great career and explains what it means to represent the county

W hen I was a youngster I supported Lancashire. Having been born in Billinge, a village on the outskirts of Wigan, to a farming family on the side of the East Lancashire Road this loyalty was probably inevitable. Even though we were living in Middlesex, where back-garden games of cricket against my brother, Alastair, were a daily occurrence, my batting line-up always contained the names of Frank Hayes, David Lloyd, Clive Lloyd, Barry Wood, Harry Pilling and Jack Simmons.

Alastair was always Middlesex. He was playing youth cricket for the county at the time and his side contained Mike Brearley, Clive Radley, Graham Barlow, Mike Gatting and Wayne Daniel. My cricketing talents were yet to be identified by Middlesex's youth coaches.

I think my allegiance changed on one of my early visits to Lord's to watch Middlesex play Lancashire in 1980. Middlesex had emerged as one of the leading teams in the country and I remember sitting in the Allen Stand – previously Q Stand – with my best mate, Stephen Williams, questioning the credentials of an old-looking man fielding in front of us. Stephen said he opened the bowling for Middlesex and that he was a top bowler. Before he had bowled a ball I begged to differ.

Yet within an hour I was eating my words. The 'old man' was Vintcent van der Bijl, the magnificent South African fast bowler and he was making short work of Lancashire's top order. Four years later it was therefore slightly ironic that Don Bennett, the great Middlesex coach, signed me for the club because he believed my bowling had van der Bijl's qualities. I had a good go but, as hard as I tried, I was never quite that good.

Coming to Lord's is one of the great attractions of following

> **I believe not owning Lord's has made Middlesex's players far humbler than many of those that play at counties that host Test matches**

Middlesex but even now many people do not fully comprehend the club's relationship with the ground and the Marylebone Cricket Club. The uncertainty is understandable because even though Middlesex have only been tenants since 1877 they have played as big a role in the ground's history as anyone. Four of the stands – Allen, Compton, Edrich and Warner – at the home of cricket are named after great Middlesex players and the club has played more cricket there than any other team.

And it is the combination of two clubs with a rich and successful history – Middlesex and MCC – along with a ground that is widely considered to be the finest in the world, which makes playing there so special. As a player I never forgot what a privilege it was to play at Lord's. To make that walk from the dressing room, down two flights of stairs, through the Long

Room and then out on to the field is unforgettable. Following the path made by all the great Middlesex and England cricketers is something no player should ever take for granted.

It is the combination of all these contrasting parts that makes playing for Middlesex such a unique and proud experience. A lack of control of what takes place in the ground is not ideal but I believe there are positives to Middlesex not owning Lord's. I believe it has made Middlesex's players far humbler than many of those who play at other counties that host Test matches. Middlesex cricketers have never been able to walk around their home ground as though they own it, because they don't. We have and always will require permission to do things there.

The club's history, however, is and should remain a source of huge pride. Counties have several roles to play. They exist to produce a strong, competitive side that provides high-quality entertainment for its members and supporters, and to produce England cricketers. In our history, on all fronts, I believe we have done a pretty good job. Only two counties – Yorkshire and Surrey – have won the County Championship on more occasions than Middlesex and in the last 50 years only Yorkshire have produced more England players.

During my career I was fortunate enough to play in two successful Middlesex teams. The first, the team I broke in to in the mid-1980s, was a collection of superstars. As a group they weren't particularly close, indeed there were very few gatherings away from cricket. Away trips were not filled with team dinners either. Players preferred to do their own thing. As cricketers, however, they were outstanding and there were occasions when the team – Graham Barlow, Wilf Slack, Mike Gatting, Clive Radley, Roland Butcher, Paul Downton, Phil Edmonds, John Emburey, Neil Williams, Norman Cowans and Wayne Daniel – was full of internationals.

The make-up of the team, of which five were of West Indian descent, one from Norfolk, one from Kent, one from Surrey and one from Zambia was rich and varied. It produced a lively dressing room. Only Gatting, Barlow and Cowans cold be considered to be products of Middlesex cricket. The composition of this side is why I do not beat myself up about the number of Middlesex-born or -produced players we have in our teams now. Yes, we want as many local boys as possible but London is such a cosmopolitan place that it is inevitable that the make-up of Middlesex's side is more varied than most.

Despite the players' individual successes and the team's cosmopolitan nature, representing Middlesex and playing at Lord's remained a big thing. Each cricketer had huge pride in the

Pride of Middlesex: Mike Gatting on the attack at Uxbridge

club and themselves. Gatting ensured this was the case and I am yet to meet a man who took more pride in representing the club than our former captain. Watching the team of the '80s go about their business was extremely beneficial for a youngster. Every player knew his role and was fit enough to do his job. They were all excellent professionals and they showed me what I needed to do to succeed.

The second Championship-winning team was in complete contrast to the first, in that it contained many products of the Middlesex system. The 1993 side contained Gatting, John Carr, Mark Ramprakash, Cowans, Williams, Fraser, Keith Brown, Richard Johnson, Paul Weekes and Philip Tufnell. Mike Roseberry developed as a cricketer in Middlesex too. As a group this side was a lot closer than that of the mid-'80s. It spent a lot of time together socially and, even now 20 years on, we remain good friends.

Lord's has provided me with many happy memories, and that is not just because of the quality of the lunches. I remember being too embarrassed to move the sightscreens at the Pavilion End on one of the first occasions I batted at the ground, my first five-wicket haul against Nottinghamshire in 1988 and, in the same season, being presented with my county cap on the dressing-room balcony during a match against Glamorgan.

The highlights at Lord's though would be winning the NatWest Trophy in 1988, being presented with the County Championship in 1993 and producing two five-wicket performances for England in Tests against India and West Indies. To see your name on the honours boards in the home dressing room is something special. Those performances will always be there.

I was fortunate to be involved in three County

Get in, Gus: Angus Fraser is congratulated on taking a wicket in 1988 by, left to right, Mike Gatting, Andy Needham, Roland Butcher and Mark Ramprakash

Championship triumphs for Middlesex. In 1985 I had very little input but those in 1990 and 1993 were special. The 1990 win came a year after England had been thumped by Australia in The Ashes. England's defeat, according to the Test and County Cricket Board, was due to sporty pitches and the seam on the ball being too big. In their wisdom the TCCB made changes to both and it produced a bat-dominated summer.

This suited Middlesex as we had good batters and bowlers. In a 22-match season five of our batsmen – Desmond Haynes, Gatting, Roseberry, Brown and Ramprakash – scored more than 1,300 runs and five bowlers – Tufnell, Emburey, Williams, Fraser and Cowans – took

more than 35 wickets. The title was won in the last game of the season, when we defeated Sussex at Hove. We had a very good evening.

The 1993 win gave me more pleasure as the season was probably the most satisfying of my career. It was the first year when the County Championship was played as a 17-match four-day competition. Again it suited our strengths. In it I returned from a career-threatening injury, regained my England place and won my third title. It was a year when players kept producing career-best match-winning displays. Emburey was the star, scoring more than 600 runs in a summer where no Middlesex player reached 1,000 and taking 68 wickets.

In June and July we had a run of six successive victories and in each match somebody produced something special. Against Somerset Haynes struck a magnificent hundred to get us over the line and against Surrey Brown scored 159 runs and Williams took six wickets. The game against Glamorgan was as good as any I played in. In their first innings Glamorgan scored 562 for 3 declared, with Viv Richards and Adrian Dale scoring unbeaten double hundreds. Gatting and Emburey then struck wonderful hundreds for us before Tufnell turned a match in a session by taking a career best 8 for 29. Carr scored 192 against Warwickshire while Emburey and Tufnell shared 15 wickets. The spin

ANGUS ROBERT CHARLES FRASER

Born: August 8, 1965, Billinge

Right-arm fast-medium bowler, right-hand batsman

- 679 first-class wickets (886 overall) at 26.41 for Middlesex 1984–2002
- 177 wickets at 27.32 in 46 Tests
- 334 one-day wickets for Middlesex
- Leading Middlesex first-class wicket-taker 1988, 1989 (best 82 wickets), 1999
- Played in three Championship-winning sides
- Two one-day trophies
- Middlesex cap 1988
- Wisden Cricketer of the Year 1996
- Middlesex benefit 1997
- Middlesex captain 2001–02
- Awarded MBE 1999
- Middlesex managing director of cricket 2009–

twins shared another 16 wickets in the next game against Hampshire. In the last Roseberry and Gatting plundered big hundreds and I took a career best 7 for 40.

The title was confirmed when we were not playing and our celebrations, during our last game of the season at Worcester, were probably a little excessive. They resulted in us losing our only four-day match of the summer.

Connecting with and highlighting Middlesex's past is something I have been very keen to do since returning to the club as managing director of cricket. Most sports clubs in England have more than 100 years of history behind them and because of this I believe sportsmen and women should take great pride in representing every team they play for, whether it is Stanmore, Middlesex or England.

Sadly, there will be many young cricketers playing in Middlesex's youth sides who are not fully aware of what the club has achieved. Some, I am sure, probably didn't know that Tufnell used to play for the club. To many he is the bloke who captains a team on *A Question of Sport* and does commentary on *Test Match Special*. Tufnell actually took over 1,000 first-class wickets and helped Middlesex win two County Championship titles.

In the past two or three years we have produced a DVD on which players, including Brearley, Gatting, Radley, Tufnell, Ramprakash, Andrew Strauss and Steven Finn talk about what it means to play for Middlesex. The film also explains the history of the club. We have also created a table outlining the characteristics we want to see in a Middlesex cricketer.

I believe the unique set of circumstances in which the club finds itself – Lord's, MCC and London – means there is a 'Middlesex way'. We will not always get it right but our responsibilities run deeper than the club. Middlesex realise there is more at stake than winning a game at all costs and we attempt to do things the right way. We want our cricketers to show pride in the club, pride in themselves and pride in the game. Most importantly we want everyone to be the best they can be. ●

THE LORD'S EXPERIENCE

Former Middlesex bowler **Simon Hughes** recalls his first impressions of the home of cricket and explains why, decades later, he still loves coming back

It is often said that Middlesex and Lord's are uneasy bedfellows and that Middlesex players never feel really at home at Lord's because it isn't theirs. I can see what they mean. To me Lord's felt more like the home of a slightly austere great uncle, full of antiques (the spectators as much as the artefacts), mysterious rooms and rather formal – a difficult place to relax properly, but unique and special and hugely inspiring all the same, and a constant in my life for over 30 years.

I arrived at Lord's for my first day as a professional cricketer on the 159 bus with my kit stuffed in two carrier bags. It was not the most auspicious arrival and I was almost refused entry to the pavilion because I wasn't wearing a tie. When I mentioned the words "Mike Brearley" I was let in with a stern "Well, mind you wear one in future". I noticed the experienced seam bowler Mike Selvey climbing the stairs wearing jeans and trainers and a T-shirt with "No Wucking Furries" printed on it but I said nothing.

It was my first time inside the pavilion and I was struck by the polished floors and the scale of the place – the wide staircases, high ceilings and endless corridors. Trying to find the dressing rooms I stuck my head round various doors. In one room an old chap in white vest and shorts was practising shots in a mirror with a funny curved racket which I later discovered was used in Real Tennis. In another an elderly man was poring over a newspaper with a magnifying glass. He grunted at the sound of the creaking door without looking up.

Eventually I found the home dressing room, identifiable initially by a loud and incessant cracking sound coming from

SIMON PETER HUGHES
Born: December 20, 1959, Kingston-upon-Thames
Right-arm fast-medium bowler, right-hand batsman

- 407 first-class wickets (466 overall) at 30.11 for Middlesex 1980–1991
- Leading Middlesex wicket-taker 1986 (63 wickets)
- Best bowling 7-35 v Surrey 1986
- 200 one-day wickets (272 overall) at 25.81 for Middlesex
- Four County Championship titles
- Six one-day trophies
- Middlesex cap 1981
- Middlesex benefit 1991

within. It could have been someone being systematically whipped in a sort of weird pre-season initiation ceremony. On peering round the door I realised it was Mike Gatting knocking two bats in by whacking them together. The dressing room was a riot of half-opened boxes of new equipment, sweaters and shirts wrapped in cellophane and 'coffins' – those huge rectangular kit bags cricketers used to use that were always groaning at the hinges and had to be humped up and down the stairs by the poor, over-worked dressing-room attendant.

Although I knew most of the players already from our pre-season 'training camp' (five days in a dodgy leisure centre in Ealing), I entered gingerly but, seeing one available hook near the window, hung my donkey jacket on it and put my bags on the floor. A player I hadn't yet met approached and said: "There'll be a lot of hard yakka before you nick my spot in the dressing room mate! Off you go down the corridor to change with the Dinky Doos" (which I soon found out was rhyming slang for 'twos'.) I did as I was told. I had this impression of county cricketers as highly-tuned athletes so was surprised shortly afterwards to see the Middlesex and England spin twins John Emburey and Phil Edmonds walking down the corridor together wearing their pads. They drove from the pavilion to the Nursery for nets.

" I was surprised to see Emburey and Edmonds driving from the pavilion to the Nursery End for nets

The rest of us, dressed in full whites – you weren't allowed on either the playing or practice area without – walked out of a side door of the pavilion, skirted round the edge of the hallowed grass, almost tip-toing for fear of damaging the revered turf, and arrived at the Nursery End. I bowled in the nets for about two hours and then, after a bit of fielding practice, retired back to the pavilion for lunch – capped players in the players' dining room, the rest of us queuing up with various taxi drivers and other plebs at the self-service counter in the Tavern pub. We returned to the nets for another two hours bowling in the afternoon before being allowed home at 5pm.

This routine continued for the next four days. On the fifth afternoon I finally got a bat. I soon regretted it. The net pitches, previously immaculate, were now quite cut up from intensive use

and a number of deliveries located my unprotected inner thigh. I had to retire to the physio's room, which contained a couch, a set of scales and boxes of crêpe bandage and tubigrip, and reeked of TCP, to have it dressed by our rather eccentric Johnny Miller who was almost blind and called everyone "mate" as a result.

That was my first week at Lord's. It was scant preparation for my first experience of playing there two months later. Leaving the dressing room to go out to bat, I was acutely conscious of the portraits of the former greats adorning the walls, the paintings of WG Grace and a stern looking Sir Don Bradman staring down as I walked out nervously to bat. The size and stature hits you as you walk down the pavilion steps and on to the manicured grass trod by all the great players for two centuries. You feel small and insignificant, a speck on a vast canvas. And soon after if you are bowled for nought as I was, you are walking back and the expressions of the legends on the wall seem to have turned darker and the good wishes of the members as you headed out turned to embarrassed silence. Most can't look you in the eye. But to have appeared in that unique arena at all gives you an amazing feeling of satisfaction.

Never mind the cricket, it's all the peripherals that were really exceptional. The lunches, prepared by the amusingly severe Nancy Doyle, were lavish. Lamb cutlets with four vegetables and chips followed by apple pie, ice cream, cream and custard was the best. The tea trolley arrived at 4.10 laden with sandwiches, scones and cream, jam tarts and those cakes with stringy bits of coconut. You were superbly looked after with a dressing-room attendant bringing you drinks and huge soft towels and running you a hot bath after play. The shower heads were the size of dinner plates. We were wonderfully pampered then at the place rightly called the headquarters of cricket and both players and the media still are.

Although I have now spent more days at Lord's as a journalist and broadcaster than I did as a player, it is those first few days there that linger longest in the memory. It was a privilege to play there then and it is still a privilege to work there now. It may not feel like home but it is the best place for cricket in the world. It helps make Middlesex the great county that it is. ●

Simon Hughes can be heard on BBC Test Match Special, Channel 5, *and ITV and read in the* Daily Telegraph. *He has a written a number of books including the award-winning* A Lot of Hard Yakka *(which covers his Middlesex career) and most recently* Cricket's Greatest Rivalry: A History of the Ashes in 10 Matches. *Follow him on Twitter @cricketanalyst*

THE MAGNIFICENT SEVEN

The sometime Middlesex out-ground at Southgate still bears the family name but the **Walkers'** influence on the establishment and early years of the club stretch way beyond that, writes **Marcus Williams**

In the way that the Graces are identified with the formative years of Gloucestershire and the Fosters with Worcestershire so too the Walkers of Southgate loom large with Middlesex. There were seven brothers, all of whom represented the county and four of whom were pivotal figures in the first six decades of the club's existence.

John Walker, the eldest, was joint vice-president – there was no president for the first two years – when the Middlesex County Cricket Club was founded in 1864 and he remained in that office until his death in 1885; his brothers VE (known as Teddy) and RD (Russy) were on the committee. For the first two seasons John and Teddy were joint captains, the latter continuing on his own until 1872 after which ID (Donny) took up the reins for the next dozen seasons. Teddy was also secretary from 1865 to 1870, treasurer from 1895 to 1906, and president from 1898 to 1906. He was succeeded by Russy who held the office until his death in 1922 ended the Walkers' direct involvement with the county.

The Walker family lived at Arnos (previously Arno's) Grove, better known in the mid-Victorian period as a sumptuous country house off Cannon Hill, Southgate, rather than, as in modern times, a stop on the Piccadilly line. Their wealth came from interests in the Taylor Walker brewery and Arnos Grove was in the family's hands from 1777 to 1918. The house is now a residential care home called Southgate Beaumont and keeps the former owners' name alive with a Walker Suite.

The boys picked up their love of cricket at school – four of them went to Harrow – and university. The three eldest boys went to Cambridge and Russy to Oxford; Donny was also due to go to Cambridge but the death of their mother caused a change of plan. Before the formal establishment of the county club a team called Middlesex, raised by John Walker, played against other counties and the remaining brothers, Alfred, Fred and Arthur, also took part in some of those games. All the Walkers represented the Gentlemen against the Players apart from Alfred, who was nonetheless a capable fast under-arm bowler.

John was the prime mover in establishing a cricket club in Southgate in 1855 and there were visits from leading teams, with thousands turning up to watch the United All England XI take on the 16 men of Southgate in a carnival atmosphere. John was also the driving force behind the establishment of Middlesex CCC and it seems that in the early years of the club the Walker family met most of the club's expenses including travel and rent of the various grounds before the eventual move to Lord's.

Probably the best player was Teddy, the fifth of the brothers; he was certainly the most stylish batsman. In 1856 he was chosen for the Gentlemen at the age of 19 and three years later, for England against Surrey, he took all ten wickets in the first innings, and 14 in the match, with his fiercely spun lobs. To this feat he added a century in the second innings leading Lillywhite's *Guide to Cricketers* to describe him at this time as "the best all-round cricketer in the world", although the boundaries of that world did not stretch far beyond England.

When the county club came into existence Teddy was still in his prime and his all-round skills were augmented by his outstanding captaincy. He took all ten wickets on two other occasions: for Gentlemen of Middlesex against Gentlemen of Kent at Maidstone in 1864 and for Middlesex against Lancashire at Old Trafford in 1865. He played his last game for Middlesex in 1877, thereafter devoting more time to the family brewing business and taking over the running of the estate after the deaths of John and Fred; but he still served the game

Good innings: RD (Russy) Walker lived until he was 80

The best player: VE (Teddy) Walker

> **When illness afflicted him in later years, Russy would be seen in his bath chair holding court in front of the old players' dressing room at the end of the pavilion**

he and his brothers loved. He was president of MCC in 1891 and fulfilled several roles for Middlesex until his death in 1906, when he left assets of nearly £1.6 million (around £146 million at modern values).

Donny, the youngest brother, spent four years in the Harrow School XI, two as captain, and played for Middlesex for 20 years, 15 of them as captain. In 1868, the year in which he scored 165 for the Gentlemen against the Players at The Oval, he was rated second only to WG Grace as a batsman. In 1883 with Alfred Lyttelton he put on 324 for the second Middlesex wicket against Gloucestershire at Bristol. They scored the last 226 runs in 105 minutes, many of Donny's 145 runs doubtless coming from his trademark drive over cover-point. After retiring from first-class cricket at the end of the 1884 season, the last Walker to play for the county, he devoted himself to coaching cricket at his old school.

Only 54 when he died in July 1898, Donny was an immensely popular figure and was accorded a three-page obituary in the following year's *Wisden*, which recalled "the flags floating half-mast high, and the genuine grief that was expressed on all sides" at the Eton v Harrow match two days after his death. It also led to Middlesex's match against Kent being postponed until the end of August to allow members of the team to attend his funeral at Christ Church, Southgate, where he was buried in the family vault.

Incidentally, the building of the church was one of many indications of the Walker family's generosity towards the local populace. The boys' father, Isaac, had given substantial funds, and the link between the church and the family was strengthened when the first vicar married their sister Anna. Moreover a private doorway was cut in the wall to allow easy access to the Walker estate! As local benefactors the Walkers were also responsible for laying out, opposite the church, the cricket ground which still bears their name and famous players were often entertained as house guests.

Russy was the sixth and most long-lived of the brothers. He was 80 when he died in 1922, the last surviving link because none of the brothers married. His friend and another Middlesex stalwart, AJ Webbe (player, captain, secretary and president between 1875 and 1936), wrote in a *Wisden* tribute: "A partial explanation of this is, I think, their wonderful attachment to each other. Never was there a more united family, and Russy was idolised up to the end of his long life by his numerous nephews

THE BROTHERS WALKER

John Walker	1826–1885
Alfred Walker	1827–1870
Frederic (Fred) Walker	1829–1889
Arthur Henry Walker	1833–1878
Vyell Edward (Teddy) Walker	1837–1906
Russell Donnithorne (Russy) Walker	1842–1922
Isaac Donnithorne (Donny) Walker	1844–1898

VYELL EDWARD WALKER

Born: April 10, 1837, Southgate
Died: January 3, 1906, Arnos Grove
Right-hand batsman, under-arm right-arm slow bowler

- 1,149 first-class runs (3,384 overall) at 17.67 for Middlesex 1859–77
- 81 wickets (334 overall) for Middlesex at 15.92
- Took all ten wickets in innings for 74 v Lancashire 1865
- Middlesex captain 1864–72

and nieces – his five sisters were all married, but alas, there is no one to perpetuate the family name."

Starting in 1861, Russy played five times for Oxford in the Varsity match, ten times for the Gentlemen against the Players and for Middlesex. In one of his later matches, a tie against Surrey at the Oval in 1876, he scored 104 with the idiosyncratic style that included dealing with bouncers by hitting them over his left shoulder and then the long-stop fielder to the boundary. Impossible to credit these days, he also batted without pads or gloves against even the fastest bowlers of the time but was reported never to have suffered serious injury.

He lived latterly at North Villa, Regent's Park (now the site of the London Central Mosque) and was a regular spectator at Lord's, where he also served as a trustee of MCC and on the MCC and Middlesex committees. When illness afflicted him in later years, he would be seen in his bath chair holding court in front of the old players' dressing room at the end of the pavilion.

His death on March 29, 1922 was truly the end of an era. The family name, of course, lives on in the Walker ground at Southgate where five of the brothers had played for a Middlesex XI against Kent in 1859 and where, between 1991 and 2011, the modern county club has played championship and one-day matches. A pithy tribute to the magnificent seven comes from *Baily's Magazine*, written on Teddy's installation as MCC president, which described them as "brewers of honest English ale as well as players of honest English cricket". Middlesex cricket is honestly in their debt. ●

Marcus Williams was a senior member of The Times *sports department for more than 30 years. He is the co-editor of* The Essential Wisden: 150 Years of Wisden Cricketers' Almanack. *He first watched Middlesex in 1956*

Trio of Walkers, left to right: VE (Teddy), John and ID (Donny)

MIDDLESEX'S FORMER GROUNDS

Cattle Market, Islington (1864-68) – the county's first ground, rented from an innkeeper named Tom Norris, was at the north-east corner of the Islington Cattle Market (later Caledonian Market) in Copenhagen Fields. A pavilion and dressing-room were built, the former building being bought by Richmond CC when Middlesex moved on from Islington after Norris began to stage other events at the ground. The first match was played in June 1864 and brought victory over Sussex by an innings and 52 runs thanks mainly to Vyell Walker's 14 wickets. There were 14 county matches in all at Islington, the last one against Surrey in August 1868.

Lillie Bridge (1871) – the condition of the Amateur Athletic Club ground at Lillie Bridge was so poor that it was not fit for first-class cricket in 1870 and Middlesex, surviving dissolution by a single vote in the winter, played only one match there in May 1871; it ended in a draw after Surrey had followed on. The ground, which was located near to West Brompton station, was deemed to be too isolated so a new home was sought.

Prince's (1872-76) – the briefly fashionable ground, in a large open space at the back of Harrods, was Middlesex's home for five seasons, starting with a two-wicket defeat by Yorkshire and concluding with a draw against Nottinghamshire. A scorecard of 1875 showed public entrances in Walton Street, Brompton, and Milner Terrace, Sloane Square, and the members' entrance in Hans Place, Belgrave Square. Cricket was only one of the activities that took place at Prince's: a roller-skating rink was popular with society ladies and cricketers were at times asked to cut down their hitting square of the wicket as it was claimed to threaten the ladies' well-being – and tea-drinking!

Middlesex had played one match at Lord's against Surrey in 1869 when they found themselves without a ground after deciding that Islington was no longer suitable. After several overtures by MCC Lord's became Middlesex's regular home ground in 1877 and has, of course, remained so ever since. **Marcus Williams**

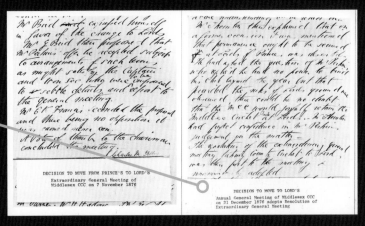

DECISION TO MOVE TO LORD'S
General Meeting of Middlesex CC[
[ember 1876 adopts Resolutio[
[ry General Meeting

DECISION TO MOVE FROM PRINCE'S TO LORD'S
Extraordinary General Meeting of
Middlesex CCC on 7 November 1876

DECISION TO MOVE TO LORD'S
Annual General Meeting of Middlesex CCC
on 21 December 1876 adopts Resolution of
Extraordinary General Meeting

INTERVIEW BY JOHN STERN

THE JOY OF SEAXE

Born in Hillingdon in 1951, celebrity astrologer and *Strictly Come Dancing* contestant **Russell Grant** is a passionate defender of the ancient county of Middlesex. He is also a long-time supporter of Middlesex CCC through his sponsorship of the Southgate festival, a colts summer league and being one of the co-founders of the Federation of Middlesex Sports. He is the author of *The Real Counties of Britain* and 20 years ago suggested – successfully – to Brentford Football Club that the Middlesex crest of three seaxes be included in their badge.

So, Russell, what came first – the cricket or the county?

Cricket came first but subconsciously I was always aware of living in Middlesex. I was born in Hillingdon but after about 18 months we moved to Harefield. My mum and dad used to get the *Daily Express* every day and I noticed that in the cricket scores there was a Middlesex County Cricket Club. I asked my dad what it meant and he said it's where we live. There were two things I used to do every day from an early age – look at the cricket scores and look at the horoscopes. But I've always kept the two things separate. The only cricketer whose stars I ever looked up was Straussy. He actually came on a sports show I did for London Weekend Television and for some unknown reason I looked at his stars, saw that he was Pisces and said he was destined for great things. My dance partner on *Strictly*, Flavia Cacace, is a Piscean as well – they've played a big part in my life!

Did you play cricket or just follow it?

No, I wasn't good at playing. I'm good at organising and scoring but not playing. My first game of cricket was Harefield against Hemel Hempstead. It was a very hot summer's day, the bees were buzzing, the butterflies fluttering. I'd have been seven or eight. Then I got involved in Harrow Town because

my mum was part of the Harrow Light Opera Society and one of her friends was a Harrow Town player so I went down to Rayners Lane and I was hooked. I ended up as their scorer. They had one of the first brick scoreboards and I was the scorer. Boy did it get hot in there. They had this huge bloke down there, Dick Harries, who looked like Charles Laughton. He would end up with crumbs all round his mouth and down his front as he ate his way through a game.

When did you get into watching Middlesex cricket?

I used to go to Lord's in the '60s when the likes of Fred Titmus, Peter Parfitt, John Murray and Eric Russell were playing. I remember the bank holiday matches against Sussex. I had a huge battle with a Somerset supporter. We were beating them and someone shouted out: "Well, you're not going to exist from next year." So I shouted back: "Get back to your cider!" I was only about 14 and this chap thought it was hilarious I was shouting at him. At that age you're even more passionate about your county. In more recent years Mike Gatting became a big favourite and David Nash was a lovely man. Then there's Tuffers, of course. We became friends in the '80s when I started off the Federation Cup. He's just fun – he's Middlesex's Robbie Savage, who's one of my closest friends since *Strictly*. I'm now his godfather!

What's behind your passion for the county of Middlesex?

I get very protective of the county and I get sick to death of people who say that Middlesex doesn't exist. Look at the facts. In 1965 the London Government Act stated that Middlesex County Council would be abolished but the county will not be and it will continue in its entirety. And it also says that sporting loyalties, affiliations and ties to Middlesex will not be affected by this Act. The bastion of counties in this country is cricket but they changed it. You have strange things like Richmond in the Middlesex League and Sunbury in the Surrey Championship. There's nothing more galling to me and many other people to see Harefield … "West London". We're 20 miles out! It was only ever a local government change and yet it's ruined our identity. The only counties older than us are Kent and Essex. But thank God we're still here and please God it never changes.

FLY THE FLAG

Russell Grant has found an ally in Eric Pickles MP, the Communities and Local Government minister. On May 16, 2011, they raised the Middlesex county flag above Pickles' department offices in Whitehall to commemorate the 200th anniversary of the Middlesex Regiment's battle against Napoleon at Albuhera. Because of the heroism of 'the Diehards', as they were known, May 16 is designated Middlesex Day.

The photograph above shows Russell with the flag on Middlesex Day 2013, flanked by local government minister Brandon Lewis (left) and John Randall, MP for Uxbridge and South Ruislip.

Pickles said: "England's counties continue to form an important part of our cultural and local identity in this country and many people remain deeply attached to their home county. This sense of pride and shared identity is one of the things that binds communities together. "Middlesex retains its place in people's memories and affections, despite attempts to wipe it off the map. The historic English counties are one of the oldest forms of local government in western Europe. Their roots run deep. And no amount of administrative reshuffling can delete these longstanding and cherished local identities." **John Stern**

❝ I GET VERY PROTECTIVE OF THE COUNTY AND AM SICK TO DEATH OF PEOPLE WHO SAY WE DON'T EXIST

WORDS BY MARCUS WILLIAMS

PLUM FINISH

Nothing warms the heart of Middlesex supporters more than victory over Surrey but **Pelham Warner**'s final Championship match provided a thrilling and unfortgettable sign-off

Middlesex have won 20 major titles, most of them in the halcyon years 1976–93, but for all the glories of that period and the golden summer of 1947 nothing can beat an earlier County Championship triumph in terms of sustained drama and excitement. The year in question was 1920 and the season reached its climax in a match which can legitimately be claimed as the greatest in the county's history. It is forever linked with the name of Pelham Warner, the revered and long-serving captain, whose last Championship match this was due to be in a career that had begun 26 years earlier.

At the start of the season Middlesex were regarded as no more than an outside bet. In 1919, during the unpopular experiment

with a two-day Championship that was introduced when cricket returned after the First World War, they had finished 13th with respectable batting but a thin bowling attack which lacked the penetration to bowl sides out twice in the shortened matches. Moreover, Warner himself, at the age of 45, had found the extended hours of the two-day games (11.30-7.30 on the first day and 11-7.30 on the second) particularly demanding and had indicated to AJ Webbe, the county secretary and his long-term mentor, his intention to give up the captaincy; but Webbe persuaded him to change his mind.

As Warner wrote later, "the gods were to smile on my decision," but at the end of July

they must have been fairly stony-faced. On July 27 Middlesex lost a thrilling match to Essex at Leyton by four runs, on the 30th Warner announced that he would retire at the end of the season, and when they went into the match against Sussex the following day they stood only sixth in the table. Because teams played varying numbers of matches positions were calculated on the percentage of points gained out of a possible maximum and Middlesex (58.18%) were a distant sixth behind the leaders Kent (78.82%) and even Nottinghamshire (66.66%) in fifth place. All, however, was set to change dramatically in the remaining nine games which were scheduled successively with only the then customary Sunday off.

"Thousands poured on to the ground": the Lord's crowd in front of the pavilion after Warner's epic triumph

The sequence began with a trip to Hove where 13 wickets for the 19-year-old leg-spinner Greville Stevens and a century by opener Harry Lee saw off Sussex by an innings; then Nigel Haig's 7 for 33 followed by JW ("young Jack") Hearne's 8 for 26 brought a nail-biting five-run win over Kent at Canterbury.

Next up were the old rivals from across the river and Middlesex produced one of their most convincing performances of the season, bowling Surrey out twice on the second day at The Oval to win by an innings and 33 runs. Hearne had an outstanding match, scoring 178 and bagging nine wickets. Fast bowler Jack Durston took seven and added another nine when Middlesex returned to Lord's and beat Nottinghamshire by nine wickets. The feature of the match was Patsy Hendren's 232, the second hundred of which came in only 55 minutes.

By now the Middlesex bandwagon was well and truly rolling, but next stop was Bradford on August 14 and a Yorkshire side that included Holmes, Sutcliffe, Rhodes and Hirst. Middlesex made only 105 in the first innings on a sticky wicket, but in another nerve-jangling finish, which the bald Warner said "turned his remaining hairs white", they squeezed home by four runs. Yorkshire's last-wicket pair had put on 53 when Stevens finally struck the stumps. The attendance over the three days was 45,000.

Middlesex were now third in the table and had become, as *The Times* reported, "serious claimants for the Championship". Their percentage had leapt to 71.25% behind Kent (73.33%) who had just lost to Surrey (72.63%), and by a twist of fate the last two of Middlesex's four remaining fixtures were against those sides.

Before that they had to face Somerset at Lord's and Warwickshire at Edgbaston and the winning run was extended to seven

" In Warner's words 'the air was charged with electricity' from the outset

matches as both were beaten comfortably. Hearne was again in outstanding form, nine wickets and the match's top score of 66 seeing off the West Country side and 215 not out plus five wickets dominating a nine-wicket win over the Midlanders.

Not only had Middlesex now moved to the top of the table but they had a new challenger in Lancashire who had leapfrogged Kent and Surrey into second place – and their final two matches were against much lower-placed opponents. On August 27 Lancashire duly beat Essex at Leyton but, after Hendren had scored 170 and 84, Durston and Stevens shared eight Kent second-innings wickets to bring Middlesex victory at Lord's by 153 runs with over an hour to spare.

And so to the final match against Surrey. With Lancashire (73.60%) more or less guaranteed victory over lowly Worcestershire, Middlesex (75.78%) had to defeat their London rivals to secure the Championship. Excitement was unprecedented for a county match at Lord's and spectators descended on St John's Wood by bus, train, cab and on foot.

The gates were closed by 3.15 on the first afternoon with people crammed into every part of the ground, up to 20 rows deep on the grass around the boundary edges and, a first, even two rows in front of the pavilion; 20,700 had paid their shilling for admission and members will have swelled the numbers further.

In Warner's words "the air was charged with electricity" from the outset. He won the toss on a fine morning and without hesitation chose to bat on a good pitch. However, the pressure of the occasion seemed to affect the Middlesex batsmen as the first three wickets fell for 35 and half the side was out for 105, including the most prolific scorers, Hearne for 15 and Hendren for 41. The bowling was tight and the fielding, led by Hobbs in the covers, gave nothing away.

Warner, however, batting at No.5 and rarely able to break the Surrey shackles, played the captain's part and grafted for more than four hours to be 70 not out at the end of the day. With good support from Stevens (53) the seventh-wicket partnership was worth 90, but by the close Middlesex were moderately placed at 253 for 8 and the title seemed to be slipping away – particularly as Lancashire had skittled Worcestershire for 124 and responded with 114 for 3.

After the Sunday break there was no let-up in the interest on Monday when 20,021 came through the turnstiles and the gates again had to be shut. Middlesex added only a further 15 runs, Warner finishing with 79, and after a few early alarms Surrey dominated the day. Hearne bagged Jack Hobbs for 24 and Durston had two more caught behind by Harry Murrell, but Andrew Sandham, surviving chances at 40 and 77, excelled with the square and late cut and went on to make an unbeaten 167. He had valuable support from Andrew Ducat and Percy Fender, the latter hitting five fours off an over from Durston, and Surrey declared at 341 for 9, a lead of 73.

Middlesex negotiated an awkward 40 minutes and reduced the arrears by 27, but few gave the home county much chance of success with one day remaining and Lancashire needing only 40 more runs with all second-innings wickets in hand to win their match.

On the final day the home dressing room was full of letters and telegrams from supporters who had not given up hope, but a wider lack of confidence in their being able to force a win was reflected in a much smaller crowd at the start … and was reinforced within the hour when Lancashire wrapped up victory over Worcestershire and were celebrating with their supporters in anticipation of securing the crown.

Back at Lord's, however, the Middlesex openers had different ideas. The exotically named amateur, Challen Hasler Lufkin Skeet, born in New Zealand but educated in London at St Paul's and an Oxford Blue,

> ## " The ground erupted and thousands poured on to the ground. Warner, who had handled his attack masterfully, was carried shoulder high from the field

PELHAM FRANCIS WARNER

Born: October 2, 1873, Port of Spain, Trinidad
Died: January 30, 1963, West Lavington, Sussex
Right-hand batsman, right-arm slow bowler

- 19,507 first-class runs (29,028 overall) for Middlesex at 37.44, 46 hundreds, 1894–1920
- 622 runs at 23.92 in 15 Tests
- Middlesex captain 1908–20
- Vice-captain in the first Championship-winning season 1903
- Captained England in ten Tests and regained the Ashes in 1903-04
- Joint-manager of the 1932-33 Bodyline tour to Australia
- Wisden Cricketer of the Year 1904, 1921' before Middx president line
- Middlesex president 1937–46
- Knighted for services to cricket 1937
- Warner Stand at Lord's opened in 1958'

and plain old pro Harry William Lee, a former Lord's groundstaff boy and son of a greengrocer, mastered the Surrey attack. Continuing until after lunch their partnership was worth 208 in 170 minutes and both scored chanceless centuries in their contrasting styles.

Lee's 108 was one of 38 first-class hundreds, including four doubles, but Skeet's 106 was the only time he reached three figures in a brief career that was most notable for his brilliant fielding and for ending when he went on colonial service to the Sudan and became a provincial governor. He could not have chosen a more opportune time to deliver his best innings.

As word spread that Middlesex were now back in the game, the ground began to fill once again, but wickets fell regularly as they pushed on to set Surrey a target. Hendren, Haig and Frank Mann, the big-hitters, failed to make a mark. It was 291 for 7 when an emotional Warner came out to a rapturous ovation from the crowd, joined by the Surrey fielders, in recognition of his final innings at Lord's. He and Stevens responded to the frenzy by adding 25 in seven and a half minutes with all manner of risky runs.

Thereupon Middlesex declared, setting Surrey a tempting target of 244 in just over three hours, and in Hobbs, Sandham,

Surrey, with seven wickets in hand, now needed another 124 in 93 minutes and the hard-hitting Fender on his way to the crease; but although his first shot, a fierce cut, threatened to break Warner's hand, he had made only a single before Durston bowled him in the next over. Middlesex struck again when Sandham was caught and bowled tamely hitting a full toss back to Hearne for an otherwise immaculate 68, At 155 for 6 Surrey were still 89 runs short with just over an hour's play left and Ducat and the tail to bat.

A missed catch from Hitch at deep square-leg by the usually reliable Hendren drew groans all round the ground and briefly threatened to stop Middlesex's progress; but Ducat was leg-before to a Hearne googly and then Hitch was bowled by a beauty from Stevens to make the score 169 for 8. Amid rising tension the last two wickets added 19 but when Stevens claimed his fifth by bowling Strudwick, Middlesex had gained a stunning victory – their ninth in a row – by 55 runs with 40 minutes to spare and were County Champions for the first time since 1903.

The ground erupted and thousands poured on to the ground. Warner, who had handled his attack masterfully, was carried shoulder high from the field, and both he and Fender made speeches from the balcony as the crowd massed in front of the pavilion at the end of an unforgettable August 31. There was no television or even radio to record the events, but the national and London newspapers gave reports of the match due prominence the next day and there were even leading articles in praise of Warner and his team. He received a host of congratulatory messages including one from the First Lord of the Admiralty who was stationed in Norway at the time. "What my feelings were, no words of mine could describe," Warner himself wrote later.

By remarkable coincidence a year later Middlesex again met Surrey at Lord's with the Championship at stake, although this time Surrey would take the title if they won whereas Middlesex had only to avoid defeat. In contrast to the great run-in of 1920 Middlesex had made the running from the start, winning their first eight matches and undefeated until July.

For two days Surrey were in the driving seat, taking a first-innings lead of 137, but Haig's five wickets cut their second innings short at 184 and Middlesex made the highest score of the match, 322 for 4, to win with unexpected ease thanks to centuries from Dick Twining and Hearne. It was another stunning victory, with a paid attendance of nearly 48,000, but the occasion has never been vested with the aura that surrounded Plum Warner's last hurrah. ●

Ducat and Fender they had the men to take up the challenge; Warner vested his side's hopes in the leg spin and googlies of Hearne and Stevens. Surrey also had the option of playing out a draw and thus denying Middlesex the Championship. It was to Fender's credit that he instructed them to keep going for the win.

Middlesex had the early fillip of Hobbs's wicket, caught for 10 by Lee at second slip via a rebound from Hendren's hands with the total 22. Howell was stumped off Stevens at 62, but then Sandham and Shepherd went after the bowling and Surrey were up with the clock as 100 was reached in 75 minutes. Another 20 runs had been added when Middlesex made a crucial breakthrough. Shepherd lofted Stevens towards the sightscreen at the Nursery End and Hendren, backtracking rapidly, caught the ball above his head a few yards inside the boundary. A roar went round the ground to acknowledge a wonderful catch.

LIVEWIRE WHO FLICKED THE SWITCH

Charles Robins profiles his father Walter whose energetic leadership reaped the ultimate reward in the unforgettable 1947 season

My father, Walter Robins, played a major part in the Middlesex story during the 20th century. He was a livewire who lived in the fast lane, not from the normal vices but because he was never fully satisfied with the present, and always prospecting his next move. One only had to travel with him on the underground where he seemed to have an encyclopedic knowledge of all the exits so that when boarding the train you arrived right opposite – in front of all the other passengers!

He was born in 1906 in Stafford where his father and two uncles played for the local club and occasionally the county with the great Sydney Barnes. So Walter and his younger brother, Vernon, spent much of their formative years watching their father and perfecting their cricketing skills.

Like so many families in that era the First World War changed everything. My grandfather was sent with the forces to East Africa and decided to stay on after the war as a regular. He was posted to London and the family duly followed in 1919. Walter, aged 13, needed to continue his education in the capital so his mother, armed with a letter of his exploits at Stafford Grammar, who he had already represented at both soccer and cricket, managed to persuade the headmaster of Highgate School to accept him on very favourable terms. This was the big break because his father was only on a Warrant Officer's pay and since the school was in the centre of Middlesex, it later provided his residential qualification to play for the county.

His time at Highgate was most successful and finished with selection for Middlesex for three games during the holidays in his last year in 1925. His headmaster was so pleased that he personally organised a special Highgate scholarship that enabled Walter to go on to Cambridge where he won blues for soccer and cricket while playing for Middlesex during the long vacations. By 1928 he had started to perfect his googly bowling.

He had a gap year in 1929, and being an impecunious amateur, this was the only full season he had with Middlesex in those early days. He made full use of it taking 162 wickets, completing the double and being selected for England. By the end of that season he found a job selling advertising space for the Nottingham furniture tycoon and cricket fanatic, Sir Julien Cahn who, by chance, was taking his own side on a tour South America that winter. Walter went on the tour and then to live in Nottingham where Sir Julien had his own ground and fixtures. While Walter played in the first two Tests against Australia in 1930 and was always on the selectors' minds for the next four seasons his commitment was to Sir Julien, and hence he had sparse availability for Middlesex.

This situation changed in 1934. Walter had by then married my mother and her father owned a Lloyd's insurance broker. His office was in the City, and he offered Walter an opportunity to sell general insurance on half-commission basis, with a fixed annual retainer. This was a wonderful chance and the family moved south to be near the action. Meanwhile, Middlesex were struggling and had run into a barren period with the 47-year-old Nigel Haig still at the helm. Finding amateurs who had the time and finance to spare but were also good enough was always difficult and with all the uncertainties in the mid-1930s candidates were indeed scarce.

Walter was by no means an obvious choice. He was well known to have a lightning-quick temper and over the years had ruffled a few establishment feathers. However, he had always been supported by Pelham Warner, and Gubby Allen was an old and reliable friend. Those two held most of the power at court so Walter was eventually invited.

ROBERT WALTER VIVIAN ROBINS
Born: June 3, 1906, Stafford
Died: December 12, 1968, St John's Wood
Right-hand batsman, right-arm leg-spin bowler

- 9,337 first-class runs (13,884 overall) at
  26.37 for Middlesex 1925–51
- 669 first-class wickets (969 overall) for
  Middlesex at 22.28
- 612 runs and 64 wickets in 19 Tests
- Did the double of 1,000 runs (1,134 at 26.37)
  and 100 wickets (162 at 21.53) in 1929
- Wisden Cricketer of the Year 1930
- Middlesex captain 1935–38, 1946–47, 1950
- Captained England in three Tests v New
  Zealand in 1937
- England selector 1946–49 and 1954;
  chairman of selectors 1962–64

The club was immediately invigorated, coming third in the County Championship in his first year, 1935, and second in the next four years, the last of which was under the captaincy of Ian Peebles who had succeeded Walter. The emergence of Denis Compton in 1936, Bill Edrich, who qualified the following year, then Jack Robertson and Sydney Brown coming to the fore in the two seasons immediately pre-war, brought added depth.

On reassembling in 1946 Peebles felt unable to continue as captain having lost the sight of an eye during a war-time bombing raid, so Walter stood again. With a very strong batting side and the bowling being carried by the pre-war trio of Jim Sims, Jack Young and Laurie Gray they again finished a close second to Yorkshire. But in 1947 they won at last, after the club's *annus mirabilis*. Walter retired happy, and although he came back to help out again at the age of 44 in 1950, this was the pinnacle of his playing career.

While MCC handled all the day-to-day office workings for Middlesex, the county appointed an honorary secretary to handle negotiations with MCC, fixtures, gate receipts, finance and remuneration for the playing staff. Walter occupied this position from 1935 to 1950 – all for no monetary reward!

He was an exceptional all-round games player. In addition to his cricket and his football for the Corinthians and Nottingham Forest, he was a noted Fives player at school, a four-handicap at golf, a hundred-break at billiards and while in Canada, where the air crews were trained during the war, he strapped his batting thigh pad across his backside, determined to compete at ice hockey with the locals. There was no game at which he did not give full attention and reckoned games were never to be conducted in silence: it was certainly not sledging, but more of a running commentary. While he did not enjoy losing he thought it to be part of education and he was always prepared to take the calculated risk.

While he was never that easy to live close to, as I found out to my chagrin on many occasions, he had no side or vanity and hated any kind of pomposity. Unfortunately, the breakneck pace at which he had lived took its toll at a comparatively young age, and sadly never allowed him to become our president. After being ill for some time he died in 1968. ●

Charles Robins played 44 first-class matches for Middlesex between 1953 and 1960. He is a former chairman and president of the club and was chairman of the cricket committee from 1974 to 1987

INTERVIEW BY JOHN STERN

GOVERNOR OF ALL THE TALENTS

Mike Brearley reflects on how, under his captaincy, Middlesex were transformed from also-rans into the premier force in county cricket.

In late June 1949 when a 16-year-old Fred Titmus made his debut for Middlesex one of his team-mates was Horace Brearley. Thirty-three years later, as Titmus was finally calling it a day after a one-off comeback at the age of 49, he was joined in retirement by Horace's son Mike whose 12-year stint as Middlesex captain had delivered three outright Championship pennants, including the first since 1947, one shared title and two one-day trophies. "I saw the father in and the son out," joked Titmus.

Titmus's appearance for Middlesex in 1982 against Surrey at Lord's was an example of the sort of lateral thinking for which Brearley's reign was renowned. Having first played for Middlesex in 1961 Brearley had been "around the edges" of the club through the 1960s while first as a student at Cambridge University then later as a lecturer in philosophy at Newcastle University.

He made his first century for the county, opening with Eric Russell, against the touring Australians in 1964, but it took him until 1973 to score a hundred in the County Championship. Before that, though, in 1971 he was invited to be captain as the club sought to improve on decade of under-achievement.

He developed a reputation for inclusivity. "He made everybody feel part of the side which I hadn't really felt before," says batsman Clive Radley. "He would ask everybody's opinion." And for enterprising, attacking cricket. "We risked losing in order to win – going all out for victory was part of Mike's philosophy," says seam bowler Tim Lamb. "Draws were use to neither man nor beast."

In 1976 he led his remodelled side to the Championship title. It was the start of an era of domination for Middlesex,

continued under the leadership of Mike Gatting, that would not end until the 1990s. Brearley became England captain in 1977 and won three Ashes series including the remarkable comeback victory in 1981 before retiring in 1982. He is a psychoanalyst and a respected writer on cricket. He was president of MCC in 2007-08 and is the current chairman of the MCC World Cricket Committee. **John Stern**

What were your impressions of the club in your early days as a player?
The club had been before that time, and to an extent still was, fairly snobbish. There was quite a class distinction. It was an interesting side: there were people who'd left school at 14 and been at boys' clubs and there were people who'd been to posh schools and universities so there was a whole social range. It was very London. There was a lot of humour, some of it quite sharp. It wasn't a kindly set-up. There was a lot of comment about the air of superiority of some of the committee. But there was also a degree of compliance. There was this curious attitude that combined both deference and scorn. Like the John Cleese thing, "I look up to him … ". I don't think that helped to produce an outstanding cricket team.

In 1965 Fred Titmus became the first professional captain, which I was absolutely in favour of. I remember the first day back at the start of the 1965 season in a freezing-cold April. There was a table in the middle of the dressing room. Leaning on it was Fred with JT Murray on one side and Peter Parfitt on the other. Fred said to the team: "If you think that because we've got a professional captain there'll be a bit of democracy round here then you can think again – won't they JT?"

JOHN MICHAEL BREARLEY
Born: April 28, 1942, Harrow
Right-hand batsman

- 15,985 first-class runs (25,186 overall) at 38.33 for Middlesex 1961–82, 29 hundreds
- Captained Middlesex to three outright Championship titles, one shared title and two one-day trophies
- 39 Tests 1976–81 including 31 as captain 1977–81
- Led England to three Ashes series wins 1977, 1978-79, 1981
- Awarded OBE 1978
- Passed 1,000 first-class runs in a season 11 times (best 2,179 in 1964)
- Middlesex cap 1964
- Middlesex captain 1971–82
- Wisden Cricketer of the Year 1977
- Middlesex benefit 1978

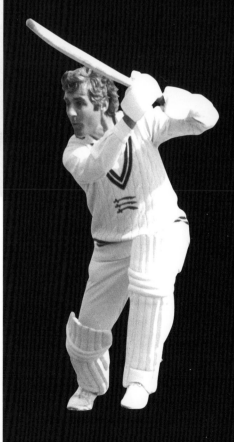

> ❝ I could be naïve. I could be earnest and theoretical instead of being practical and down to earth

And what did the senior players make of you?

I was uppity, from university, probably thought I knew more than I did and was cut down to size – but I wasn't the only one. There wasn't much sense that your opinion was welcomed until you'd played ten years as a capped player or played 20 or 30 times for England. It wasn't conducive to a good team spirit.

How did you become captain?

It coincided with me deciding I didn't want to be a university lecturer for the rest of my life. Someone on the committee asked me if I might be interested and I said I might. I liked the idea of the stimulus of being captain but there were times in those first two or three years when I wondered if I should carry on. We weren't doing very well, I wasn't scoring many runs and there was a certain amount of hostility and bad feeling. It was hard.

What were the key things that needed to change?

I realised two things – one was that we had to get some quicker bowlers in and secondly we had to become a club that people would want to play for. I thought that players from other counties weren't attracted by the idea of moving to Middlesex.

Fred carried the bowling. After 45 minutes' play you'd find that the opposition were 50 for no wicket then Fred would come on and bowl two or three maidens and get you back on terms.

We tried to get Norman McVicker from Warwickshire but he didn't come. We got Mike Selvey who was unhappy at Surrey and was a Londoner. He was an excellent fast-medium swing and seam bowler who was pivotal to the side for a decade. Allan Jones was also absolutely key. But he was a gamble because he'd fallen out with Sussex then he'd gone to Somerset and fallen out with them too. Brian Close [the Somerset captain] was alleged to have said: "Ian, Viv, Joel … lovely lads – but that bloody Jones!" He was about to emigrate to New Zealand. But we knew he could bowl and he could bowl quick.

And what about the atmosphere in the dressing room?

When I was made captain I did try to change the attitude in the dressing room. I had some sympathy with the younger players which meant I probably didn't have sufficient sympathy with the older players. They were to an extent suspicious of me, with some cause. I had been this part-time cricketer who'd been to university and thought I knew a thing or two but hadn't had much success for Middlesex. I could be naïve – when I was first captain I remember looking up the previous year's *Wisden* to see who had got certain opposition players out. That was just stupid. As if you could learn something from that. I could be earnest and theoretical instead of being practical and down-to-earth.

When did things start to improve?

We got to two one-day finals in 1975. We lost them both but

"Stimulating and provocative": Phil Edmonds bowling against Lancashire in 1982

> ❝ **Phil Edmonds's nickname when he first came into the side was 'Margaret' – leader of the opposition**

things were starting to get a bit better. The thing about success is it's catching. As a team you don't expect to win unless you start to win and you can easily expect to lose. The habit of winning is very important. Then we won the Championship in '76 in part because it was a hot, late summer and the pitches turned. We had Philippe Edmonds, Titmus and John Emburey and also Norman Featherstone who was a decent off-spinner. Selve and Allan Jones plus three spinners; and it was a decent batting side. We also had a very good second XI side, for which much credit goes to the coach Don Bennett. Players like Graham Barlow, Embers, Gatt and Ian Gould were coming through looking ready for the first team.

How would you assess Phil Edmonds?

He was a terrific cricketer. It's well known that we had our difficulties but we also had enjoyable conversations. He was stimulating and provocative and probably I was too. We quite enjoyed each other at times. His nickname when he first came into the side was 'Margaret' – leader of the opposition. That wasn't me, that was the team. It was a tough environment.

I felt about Philippe that he didn't really learn. He had such talent but he never became a better batsman, he became, if anything, worse. And his bowling didn't really develop the way that John Emburey's did. John was a lesser cricketer when he first played for Middlesex but by the end he was as effective a batsman and a more versatile bowler. Philippe could always bowl a ball to get a top batsman out but he was less shrewd in bowling to tailenders, and less patient. The other thing about him was he wasn't as confident as I thought he was. He had an air that made me feel stupid but I came to see eventually that this was often his way of expressing his own uncertainty. When I wanted him to bowl slower, for example. He also went through that terrible time when he lost it, as so many left-armers have done. That was very painful. He was bowling high full tosses and double bouncers. It meant he couldn't bowl as a spinner, he was bowling as a medium-pacer not trying to spin it. He was also a brilliant fielder. I don't think I handled him very well.

You beat Surrey to the Championship and the Gillette Cup in 1980. Was there a fierce local rivalry?

Sussex and Surrey were two of the teams that we had good battles with. There was a game at The Oval on a relaid pitch when Sylvester Clarke was lethal and so were Wayne Daniel and Vince van der Bijl. Grahame Clinton had ten stitches in his forehead. Sylvester was as quick as anyone. I quite liked him as a bloke, though. He had a way about him, he'd give you this slightly quizzical look, like Andy Roberts did, that seemed to say: "You think you're going to bat against me, man?"

There was a memorable B&H game against Sussex in the same season in which we batted first and made 195. It was probably about par. The pitch wasn't easy, it was cloudy and they had good bowlers. Imran Khan wasn't shy of bowling bouncers. When he came in to bat I brought Wayne back on because he didn't like Wayne. Then he started to complain about the light and about bouncers from Wayne. I thought this was a bit rich given it was the same light that

SEASON OF SUCCESS: 1976

THE START OF SOMETHING SPECIAL

Middlesex won the County Championship outright for the first time since 1947. "We didn't have any stars, it was a good side that played well together," says Mike Selvey, who was one of four bowlers to take more than 60 Championship wickets.

It was a season that "changed the club completely", according to young wicketkeeper batsman Ian Gould, who was one of four keepers used by Middlesex in the immediate aftermath of John Murray's retirement. Indeed, Murray was asked to come back but declined.

Middlesex used three keepers in one afternoon during their victory over the touring West Indies. Gould was away on a Young England tour and the first choice Nigel Ross was injured. His replacement Rodney Kinkead-Weekes broke a finger during the match and was replaced by Mike Brearley, who in turn was replaced by Roland Butcher after hurting his back.

At the end of July Middlesex beat Nottinghamshire to go top of the table. They acquired a small first-innings lead helped by nightwatchman Tim Lamb's only first-class fifty. "I was absolutely shattered," he says, "and it must have affected my ability to bowl [Lamb didn't bowl in the second innings]. When I was in the 40s I chipped a ball riskily over the infield. Bob 'Knocker' White, ex-Middlesex, was the bowler and asked me if I'd ever got a fifty before. I hadn't and he said: "Well, don't throw it away now, son." That summed up the way the game was played in those days. It was nice."

Middlesex needed 201 to win in two hours and 20 minutes, and then 114 from the last 20 overs. Roland Butcher, who was dropped twice, put on 97 for the fifth wicket with Phil Edmonds who was run out with only four to win.

Five points were needed from the final match at The Oval and having picked up three bowling points in Surrey's first innings, the title was secured at 4pm on the second day when it emerged that Gloucestershire had failed to take full bowling points against Derbyshire. Middlesex were batting and Selvey remembers: "Allan Jones and I went down to the bar – in the middle of the innings – and had a couple of pints. But then a couple of wickets went down and I had to go out and bat. I played like God. I was only in 10 or 15 minutes and got 29. I was playing shots all over the place, p***** as a parrot. I'd obviously been too buttoned up before!" Middlesex won the game by five wickets thanks to an unbeaten sixth-wicket stand of 140 between Edmonds and Norman Featherstone who had come together at 36 for 5.

It was, as Selvey says, a real team effort. Left-hander Graham Barlow emerged as leading run-scorer with 1,282 at 49.30 while both Mikes, Brearley and Smith, topped 1,000 Championship runs. Selvey, Jones, Edmonds and Fred Titmus all took more than 60 wickets but it was South African-born all-rounder Featherstone who topped the averages with 32 wickets at only 14.75 with his under-rated off-breaks. He was the man who, according to Gould, "came alive in August". **John Stern**

Make the iconic ground of Lord' YOUR HOME

BECOME A MEMBER OF MIDDLESEX COUNTY CRICKET CLUB

ALREADY A MEMBER?
INTRODUCE A FRIEND AND SAVE ON YOUR MEMBERSHIP SUBSCRIPTION

* FREE ENTRY TO ALL MIDDLESEX HOME MATCHES AT LORD'S & OTHER HOME GROUND
* PRIORITY APPLICATION FOR INTERNATIONAL TICKETS AT LORD'S
* WATCH ALL MIDDLESEX MATCHES FROM THE FAMOUS LORD'S PAVILION

middlesexccc.com/membership | 020 7289 1300

SEASON OF SUCCESS: 1977

DROPPED POINTS AND CHIP SHOTS

Middlesex shared the County Championship with Kent and exorcised the ghosts of their two one-day final defeats of 1975 by winning the Gillette Cup (see page 91). "It was a very strange season," says Mike Selvey. It ended with Middlesex at Blackpool needing two more first-innings runs to secure a batting point and with it the title. Selvey was at the crease facing Lancashire's legendary off-spinner, 'Flat' Jack Simmons. "I got sawn off," Selvey says. "Flat Jack was bowling round the wicket and got me lbw with this big swinging arm ball which I tried to turn to leg – it was a terrible decision."

There were many other oddities, not least Ian Gould's dressing-room antics. "This was the year that I made my name a little bit," he says. "But I made my name early in the season for the wrong reasons. We had a period where we just didn't get on the field because it rained and rained. The boys had a bet that I couldn't hit a nine-iron out of the dressing-room window off a clothes brush. I did – and managed to land it right in the middle of the Test wicket, much to the consternation of Jim Fairbrother, the groundsman."

Back on the field, in the space of just over a month through to the end of August, Middlesex were involved in enough peculiar happenings to last a season, or indeed several seasons. In late July they finished 23 runs short (63 for 7 chasing 86) in a run-chase against Gloucestershire but were aggrieved because the umpires' miscalculation had deprived them of an over.

Two matches later at Sheffield Middlesex were denied their full complement of bowling points because three Yorkshire batsmen had retired hurt. "It's anomalous really and you do count these things up at the end of the summer," says Selvey. "It was a pretty flirty pitch and the Yorkies, being brave, were all getting in behind it. John Hampshire got hit right on the point of the elbow by Wayne Daniel – it was horrible. Arnie Sidebottom broke his arm; Allan Jones broke Richard Lumb's finger and Bluey Bairstow couldn't move because he had haematomas all over his legs and had to go to hospital."

Then in early August came an astonishing victory over Surrey in a game where only two overs' play were possible on the first two days. Selvey recalls: "In those days if you didn't start by tea on the second day it became a one-innings match and you played for reduced points. We started two overs before tea on the second day, had those two overs then it rained again. So now it was a 'proper' game again. In those days I travelled down to Lord's by train and I was standing on Wolverton station thinking about how we could still win it. It sounded simple: Wayne and I bowl them out, we declare, then Wayne and I bowl them out again and we knock them off. We started talking about it. The pitch was a bit damp. Wayne and I did bowl them out – for 49."

"When they were eight down," remembers Mike Brearley, "I asked the umpires if we could forfeit our first innings. They didn't know so I went off the field to ask Donald Carr [of the TCCB]. We weren't allowed so we batted for one ball."

Surrey were all out for 89 in their second innings – Monte Lynch bagging a pair before lunch – and Middlesex won by nine wickets.

In mid-August Middlesex faced Somerset in the Gillette Cup semi-final at Lord's. But because of rain it was completed only on the sixth scheduled day. The delay necessitated moving Middlesex's Championship match, also against Somerset, to Chelmsford, their first home game away from Lord's since they played at Hornsey in 1959.

Opener Mike Smith, later the first-team scorer, led the way with 1,226 runs. Brearley pays this tribute: "He was a very good player. He was thoughtful. In his early days he used to get put down by the senior players partly because he was funny and, a bit like David Gower, he would make some crack just when you didn't want to hear it. He was philosophical and thoughtful." **JS**

we'd had all day and he'd bowled at least as many bouncers as Wayne ever bowled. I was nervous that umpire Jack van Geloven would be swayed so I got involved. I marched up to him and said: "Your problem, Imran, is that you can't get it up." He came towards me with his bat raised and Gatt, who was at mid-on, thought he was going to hit me with his bat so ran up and pinioned me from behind which showed to the press that something was going on. It was the sort of atmosphere you sometimes got in Ashes matches. There was a rivalry, a history and clashes of egos.

You had a reputation for innovative captaincy. Was it born out of a will to win or a sense of fun?

I certainly thought they [innovations] would be effective although there was an element of fun too. To have a strange field is partly because you think the ball might go there but also to make the batsman think you're doing something that you might not be doing. I think I was inventive in that way.

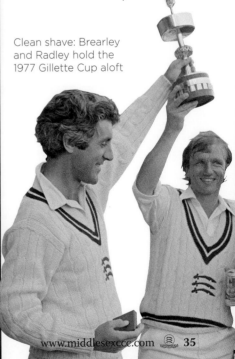

Clean shave: Brearley and Radley hold the 1977 Gillette Cup aloft

SIMPLY THE BEST

"I can't think that there have been many better bowling sides in the history of the County Championship," reckons Mike Selvey, "and given that it's a surprise we didn't win more easily. We were very good that year." Middlesex won the Championship in what *Wisden* described as "virtually a one-horse race", the Gillette Cup (see page 91-92) and reached the semi-finals of the Benson & Hedges Cup and came third in the 40-over John Player League.

Anticipating that their star fast bowler, Wayne Daniel, would be picked on West Indies' tour of England, Middlesex recruited a 32-year-old South African, Vintcent van der Bijl, to replace him. When Daniel didn't make the tour Middlesex suddenly had an unbeatable combination on their hands: van der Bijl took 85 Championship wickets at 14.72, Daniel 67 at 21.70. Forty-nine of van der Bijl's 85 wickets were bowled or lbw and Middlesex accrued 80 out of a possible 88 bowling bonus points through the season.

Van der Bijl was not a professional cricketer and had just joined the paper company Wiggins Teape. He had already turned down an approach from Glamorgan but it emerged that his new boss, Derek Smith, was a Middlesex supporter. Permission for six months' leave was sought and granted and the platform laid for one of the greatest single-season performances in county cricket history.

"We had a magical time," remembers van der Bijl, who is now the umpires and referees manager for the ICC. "My wife Bev and I brought our young daughters over and although they went to school in London the headmaster allowed us to take them all over the country. He viewed it as a great education. That was the privilege of playing cricket; it was not just the playing itself.

"I learned so much about everything, including my bowling. Anyone can bowl an away-swinger, but I honed my skills – I really learned how to bowl a yorker for example – because I was playing so much and with and against so many different people, who just lived for cricket, and loved to talk about the game. I absorbed so much. I went back to South Africa and had the very best season of my career.

"I had heard a lot about county cricket from Barry Richards and Mike Procter. They told me that some days I would be exhausted. I think there was one period of 21 days when I bowled every day. We ended up in Taunton bowling to Sunil Gavaskar and I was exhausted. Brearlers wasn't very happy with me, walked down the wicket to me to give me a jolt, and said 'I'm thinking of bringing John Emburey on for a bit of pace!'

"I know there have been some great captains around the world but if anyone was better than Brearlers I would love to have played under him. He was like an intellectual realist. He loved the intrigue of life and the interaction with people. That's what inspired him. He opened thoughts in us, experiences that were lasting and encouraged us to explore ourselves. He challenged what we were thinking and within that absorbed and accepted all individuals in the group. He had that special talent and moulded us into a cohesive unit.

"A good example is Roland Butcher (below) – 'Hoover' as he was known because anything within the yards of him in the field got sucked into his path. Brearlers opened Roland up. We had a period where we hadn't lost a game for two months and then we suddenly lost two 40-over games in a row. Brearlers asked every individual in the group what was wrong. Roland said that we had already built the mantelpiece for the four trophies we were going to win. Brearlers used that in the next team talk which gave Roland huge confidence in himself and within the group. He then went and scored two big hundreds against Hampshire and Yorkshire and ended up on an England tour to West Indies at the end of that season."

In addition to the quick bowlers' contributions in the Championship, John Emburey took 61 wickets while Mike Brearley (1,282 runs) and Clive Radley (1,248) led the way with the bat. **JS**

One off: Vince van der Bijl on his way to ten wickets in the match against Derbyshire in 1980 at Uxbridge – Middlesex's first game there

Against Yorkshire you famously placed a helmet on the leg side when Phil Edmonds was bowling. What was the background to that?

I think it was my idea but it might have come from Phil or the side, I don't remember. There were lots of ideas bubbling away. It was like an argumentative home but constructive, mostly. Philippe liked the idea too and entered into it. Yorkshire were blocking solemnly so we left the whole of the leg side empty and put the helmet at short leg. There was lots of chat within the hearing of the batsmen. "Go on, look you could have five extra runs." Then we started moving it as if it were a fielder: "Shall we have him at mid-wicket?" "Can you ask him to move a bit squarer?" The batsmen [Jim Love and Richard Lumb] were somewhat bemused. Yorkshire were very proper – you had to play the game in a certain way. The authorities banned it after that, probably rightly.

In 1980 you signed Vince van der Bijl who played a hugely significant part in arguably Middlesex's most successful ever season. What do you remember?

I remember being suspicious of the signing of Vintcent, wondering whether we wanted a white South African. He became one of my best friends! I was worried it would upset the balance of the team but Vince was an unbelievably good cricketer and a terrific member of the side. He also changed the culture of the side. Part of that sharp humour, which still existed, was that you wouldn't generally take the blame yourself. But he would always take the blame himself. He'd say things like: "We lost that match because of the two half-volleys I bowled at the start." He would say this with complete sincerity. He was a lovely bloke, a great team man and a fantastic bowler. He was 6ft 7in and probably Jimmy Anderson's pace. He swung it away with bounce and accuracy. He hit the bat very hard and he would bowl all day.

> **" I remember being suspicious of the signing of Vintcent, wondering whether we wanted a white South African. He became one of my best friends!**

Title on a plate: Brearley says thanks and farewell to van der Bijl

At the other end you had Wayne Daniel who was a wonderful county cricketer (as well as a Test cricketer, of course). He was very funny at times. I'm not sure he was always on time but he was always smart. Most of us thought about cricket during the day and dreamt about women at night; Wayne would think about women during the day and dreamt about cricket. He bowled exceptionally fast against Lancashire, driven by a desire to prove a point to Clive Lloyd. There was a game in 1978 at Lord's – which I didn't play in because it was just before a Test but was watching – when he got Clive out and had Lancashire 11 for 3. But then he came off the field, having damaged his hamstring and we were all terrified. He came in and said: "That is the end, the final end of Wayne Daniel." Occasionally he would refer to himself in the third person, as Viv Richards used to.

> **" It was lively, humorous and passionate. It became a very enjoyable team to play for – we expected to win**

How would you assess the man-management side of your captaincy?

I didn't do things very well with regard to Philippe or the senior players before that. I didn't understand their position or confront the situation properly when it needed to be. That was a weakness. I was better with the younger players so when they came through I had more rapport with them. But I had no hesitation in being rough with them, some things I'm not proud of, but on the whole it was accepted.

I think I helped Roland Butcher who could get hurt by the joshing and the teasing. Racial attitudes were probably not completely absent. I encouraged him to be more aggressive and more forthcoming, rather than just withdrawing into himself and getting resentful. He was a terrifically talented batsman and he would occasionally change a match but I told him that he wasn't aggressive enough in defence, that his defence was a bit limp. It had more to do with style, Bajan style. I used to drive him round the country and one day he said he could see that everyone else had their own way of being aggressive, whether it was Fred getting angry if people didn't stop the singles or Embers going red in the face as yet another lbw was turned down.

Final farewell: Brearley leaves the field for the last time at Worcester in 1982 having hit the winning runs in a ten-wicket victory during which Middlesex secured the Championship

When you reflect on your Middlesex career as a whole, what do you remember most?
I think about those needle matches where there was rivalry but also respect. That was the best of county cricket. I also think about how long it took me to become a decent batsman. I hadn't scored a Championship hundred before I became captain or for two or three years after that. It's shocking really. I learned so slowly. So I regret certain things. But I also remember fondly the good innings that I played. I scored a hundred against Derek Underwood on a wet wicket at Canterbury which was quite something. And I scored 91 on that lethal pitch at The Oval against Sylvester Clarke. I was out hit wicket of all things, bowled by Intikhab Alam. I went down the wicket and hit the ball into my calf and it rolled back towards the stumps. As I tried to stop it hitting the wicket I knocked them all over.

Overall I remember the time with great affection. The Middlesex team was lively, humorous and passionate. It became a very enjoyable team to play for – we expected to win.

There are so many people – far too numerous to mention – who played huge roles in Middlesex cricket during my time there: not just players but members of the committee, chairs of the cricket committee and selectors as well. ●

SEASON OF SUCCESS: 1982

FITTING FAREWELL

Middlesex won their third outright Championship title under Mike Brearley in his final season. They also reached the semi-finals of the NatWest Trophy, the quarters of the Benson and Hedges and finished second in the John Player League. They were unbeaten in all forms of the game until the middle of June and in mid-August led the Championship by 47 points. Leicestershire pegged that advantage back to only two before Middlesex clinched the title at Worcester. Appropriately, Brearley hit the winning runs in a ten-wicket victory. His final match at Lord's had been the 58-run victory over Surrey in which Fred Titmus was recalled to play at the age of 49 (see page 71). In the Championship four batsmen (Mike Gatting, Wilf Slack, Brearley and Roland Butcher) passed 1,000 runs while John Emburey took 74 wickets and Wayne Daniel and Phil Edmonds both took 71. **JS**

MIDDLESEX CLUB CAPTAINS

1864–72	VE Walker
1873–84	ID Walker
1885–98	AJ Webbe
1898	AJ Webbe and AE Stoddart
1899–1907	G MacGregor
1908–20	PF Warner
1921–28	FT Mann
1929–32	NE Haig
1933–34	NE Haig and HJ Enthoven
1935–38	RWV Robins
1939	IAR Peebles
1946–47	RWV Robins
1948–49	FG Mann
1950	RWV Robins
1951–52	WJ Edrich and DCS Compton
1953–57	WJ Edrich
1958–60	JJ Warr
1961–62	PI Bedford
1963–64	CD Drybrough
1965–67	FJ Titmus
1968	FJ Titmus and PH Parfitt
1969–70	PH Parfitt
1971–82	JM Brearley
1983–97	MW Gatting
1997–99	MR Ramprakash
2000	JL Langer
2001–02	ARC Fraser
2002–04	AJ Strauss
2005–06	BL Hutton
2007–08	ET Smith
2009–10	SD Udal
2010–13	NJ Dexter

MAN IN THE MIDDLE

Only Patsy Hendren has scored more for runs for the county than **Mike Gatting** whose leadership by example made Middlesex the team of the '80s. **John Stern** interviewed him

No one surely embodies modern Middlesex as much as Mike Gatting, and few have given such unstinting, unconditional service to the county. Born in Kingsbury, nurtured at Brondesbury, he has been batsman supreme, useful medium-pacer, captain and coach. And now, fittingly, he presides over Middlesex's landlords in a year of great significance to both clubs.

There are many archetypal images of Gatt: the skipper's double teapot in the slips; the bearded grin as he holds another glittering trophy aloft; the square cut lashed to the fence; the more delicate paddle round the corner before those treetrunk thighs start pumping towards the non-striker's end. Or the current incarnation: the blazered administrator – but still playing occasionally – with the greying goatee, twitching at the sides with a friendly, slightly mischievous, smirk. But whether batting, marshalling his troops or delivering grassroots projects, Gatting leaves nothing in the dressing room. Everything he does, everything he has ever done has been imbued with honest, unaffected endeavour and devotion to the game.

Having risen quickly, under the tutelage of Ted Jackson, to Brondesbury's first XI, the 15-year-old Gatting was invited by coach Don Bennett for Wednesday night winter nets at Finchley. "It was incredible," says Gatting. "Suddenly I was facing Mike Selvey, Keith Jones and Martin Vernon – they swung the ball, at pace. The surface was concrete under lino. It was sink or swim.

"It was made clear that you had to learn and for a couple of years I kept notes on all my innings: how I got out and what sort of pitch it was. I couldn't play off-spinners when I started.

I couldn't play an on-drive, it either went straight or through square leg. I spent a whole winter with Don sorting out my on-drive. Four months later he was still bowling to me. I said: 'Well, I want to get it right Don'. He said: 'If I'd known it would take that long I wouldn't have bloody offered.'"

Along with the likes of Graham Barlow, John Emburey and Ian Gould, Gatting was part of the hugely successful second XI side that won the Warwick Pool Under-25 competition in three successive years from 1972–74. Times were changing and so was the make-up of Middlesex's side. "The introduction of Gatting and Gould in 1975 made the dressing room noisier and cheekier – it was a breath of fresh air," says Emburey.

Gould and Gatting struck up a lifelong friendship despite their opposing tastes in north London football teams. "Yeah well, he's always been Tottenham – that's his problem," says 'Gunner' Gould. "We had a great laugh. I've never had a better mate than Gatt. He's a very loyal and trusted friend. But I'm horrified to see he's now president of MCC!"

Gatting and Gould, who years later formed Middlesex's coaching team, made their first-class debuts in successive matches in 1975. During Gould's debut at Trent Bridge, Gatting's second appearance, Gatt received an unexpected initiation into the slightly anarchic world of county cricket. "Essex were playing Derby at Ilkeston and they were staying in the same hotel as us in Nottingham. It had been raining and a few people thought there wouldn't be any play the next day. Gunner went out drinking with JK Lever and some of the Essex lads while I went to bed. At one point I woke up, thinking I'm hearing rain and it's Gunner peeing in my shoes.

" I was hopefully fairly honest, sometimes a bit gullible in those days – probably still am

well and I didn't get in the side," Gatting remembers. "The only way I got back in was to open with Mike Smith when Brears went off to a Test. I was run out a couple of times by Mike and ended up at Scarborough being told I wasn't playing. So I had to go and play in the second team with my brother, Steve, at Roehampton against a South African under-21 side. I was batting with my brother, looking after him like some old mother hen, and at one point he asked Don Bennett to have a word and tell me to shut up because he couldn't concentrate. I think I got a hundred but it was one of those moments in your life when you think, 'Next time you get back make sure you don't lose it this time. Don't take it for granted.'"

As the years passed, the return from international duty was a pleasure to be savoured. "I could never have coped with not coming back to play for Middlesex straight after a Test," he says. "This was going back to playing with your mates and having fun. Test cricket was hard. You tried to enjoy it but some enjoyed it more than others. Playing for Middlesex was like playing weekend cricket at your club when you're 13 or 14. That's why it took me so long [for England] because Test cricket wasn't like that."

Welcome to county cricket! It wouldn't have been so bad if my socks and wallet hadn't been in there as well."

Gatting's batting talent – and as a bowler – was there for all to see but, just as he would also find when he later played for England, delivering the big innings proved elusive. In 1977 he was dismissed 11 times between 50 and 82 but still reached 1,000 runs and was picked on England's tour of New Zealand and Pakistan. His maiden first-class century came in August 1978, against Yorkshire, in his 110th innings. His second, in the manner of London buses, came in his next innings against Derbyshire.

In 1979 he was part of England's World Cup squad though the aftermath taught him a valuable lesson. "When I came back to Middlesex Roland Butcher was playing

Cheeky: keeper-batsman Ian Gould

MICHAEL WILLIAM GATTING

Born: June 6, 1957, Kingsbury

Right-hand batsman, right-arm medium-pace bowler

- 28,411 first-class runs (36,549 overall, 94 hundreds) for Middlesex at 52.80, 77 hundreds, 1975–98, second only to Patsy Hendren
- 4,409 runs at 35.55 in 79 Tests; 2,095 runs in 92 ODIs
- 2,150 first-class runs for Middlesex in 1984
- Second-most Middlesex hundreds (77)
- Most Middlesex one-day runs (12,029)
- Passed 1,000 runs in a season 19 times (best 2,257 1984)
- 129 first-class wickets at 28.29 for Middlesex
- Middlesex cap 1977
- Middlesex captain 1983–97
- Three County Championship titles as captain
- Five one-day titles as captain
- Captained England to Ashes victory 1986-87
- Wisden Cricketer of the Year 1984
- Middlesex benefit 1988, 1996
- Middlesex director of coaching 1999–2000

" Gatting and Gould made the dressing room noisier and cheekier – it was a breath of fresh air

Like many English batsmen before and since, Gatting benefited from the harsh exposure to Australian grade cricket. His 1979-80 winter at Balmain in Sydney brought him the club record for run-scoring and valuable confidence "in a tougher environment away from home". On his return the hundreds began to flow. He scored two more in the Championship-winning year of 1980, three more the following year then in the 1982 Championship triumph he topped Middlesex's averages with 1,273 runs at 67.00 and five hundreds.

With his batting prowess well established, he found himself assigned to other duties as well. Mike Brearley had retired and a new captain was required. Phil Edmonds had been vice-captain and coveted the top job but Emburey had replaced him as No.2 in the winter of 1981. Embers thought he was destined to take over from Brearley but was demoted for going on the rebel tour to South Africa.

"It wasn't straightforward, let's put it that way!" says Gatting. "I got a phone call from Don [Bennett] who said, 'What do you reckon?' 'Yeah love to', then I heard a bit about the politics. Don said they had planned to give it to Embers for a year to

see how he did and then to me for another year, which seemed a strange idea. I didn't care whether I was captain. I just wanted to gets runs for Middlesex.

"I had a chat with Embers and Rad and one or two of the senior guys. We had a few problems with Philippe as we were always going to. He was upset on many fronts – not playing enough for England and not being Middlesex captain, the reasons for which went hand in hand. I said to him in front of everybody, 'Come on Philippe, we don't need any of this. I can't help the fact I've been made captain. It's a great honour and I'll do it the best I can. If I was a player and you were captain I wouldn't be doing this to you. You're a senior player. I want your help. You're a great player and you should be helping us to be a better side."

Surely the prospect of replacing Brearley was a daunting one? "One good thing was that everyone knew I wasn't going to be Mike Brearley," says Gatting. "I hadn't been to university. I was just me. They knew what they needed to know. I was hopefully fairly honest, sometimes a bit gullible in those days – probably still am. Then it was a question of using the pieces on the chess board, and using Rad to help get people on side. Communication was really important. Brears allowed everyone to say their piece and we carried on with that – we didn't shut the dressing room down. It made for a very feisty environment. Embers and I had some real good set-tos."

In Gatting's first year Middlesex finished second in the Championship, reached the semi-finals of the NatWest Trophy and won the Benson and Hedges Cup after an astonishing comeback against Essex. This was Gatting's third Lord's final and he would play in four more, losing only one in 1989, but curiously never made more than 37. "I got in a couple of times but didn't get any runs and, yes it did bother me," he says. "I was probably more worried about the team and other things rather than my batting."

These were minor stains on a batting record that was in otherwise prolific health. In 1984, when Middlesex finished third in the Championship and won the NatWest Trophy, Gatting became the county's first batsman since Jack Robertson in 1952 to pass 2,000 first-class runs in a season. His scoring spree included a career-best 258 against Somerset at Bath and six other centuries.

The following summer brought Gatting's first Championship as captain despite five Middlesex players being called upon at various points in the victorious Ashes series, during which Gatt made his first Test hundred at home. "We had a lot of good players," he says. "Every time we seemed to lose a bowler, someone else seemed to come along – Yozzer [Simon Hughes] was magnificent; Norman Cowans; Nelly [Neil Williams]; Gussy came along and Wayne was still there."

Gatting identifies Wayne Daniel's retirement in 1988 as the point "when the era started to end and it became more difficult". Yet he still raised two more Championship pennants in 1990 and 1993, a testament to the influence of Desmond Haynes, who arrived in 1989, the emergence of Mark Ramprakash, Angus Fraser and Phil Tufnell, and to the inceased availability of himself and Emburey following the second, ill-advised rebel tour of South Africa in early 1990.

Another rich harvest in 1994 (1,389 Championship runs at 60.39), the fourth year in a row that Gatting was Middlesex's leading run-scorer, earned him an unexpected recall at 37 to England colours for the tour to Australia.

"It was when I came back from that tour that I was aware something needed to change," he says. "I thought I'd give it another year. Gussy was a lynchpin and Embers just kept going. There was Owais Shah – 'Acey', what a talent but was he responsible enough? There was a trio of Jamie Hewitt, David Nash and Shah. They could have been three lynchpins but they all lacked that intensity. I couldn't get at those guys. I handed it over to Ramps and he got frustrated as well. Did we go wrong or did those guys not have enough desire?" Gatting's foray into management as director of coaching, following his playing retirement in 1998, was brief and in August 2000 he left the club along with coach Ian Gould.

As Gatting sits in the ECB board room reflecting on his truly distinguished career, it is not the innings or personal successes that he picks out when asked for his highlights. "Just playing in a side where we had fun," he says. "People came in and out of the side but we still managed to win. From within our own areas – and beyond – we got some good people. To captain Middlesex was a great privilege and to be competitive for that period of time, to know that if you play somewhere near your best you are going to be close to the top or in a final. To play with all those great players – to captain them – was a highlight in itself, outstanding." ●

John Stern is editor at large of All Out Cricket *and a former editor of* The Wisden Cricketer. *He has been a Middlesex member since 1985*

SEASON OF SUCCESS: 1985

WHERE THERE'S A WILF THERE'S A WAY

Showered and changed, Wilf Slack (below) approached the Grace Gates, beaming ("that water-melon grin", as Mike Selvey put it) with a sweater hung around his relaxed shoulders. An unbeaten double century against the Australians might not have contributed directly to the Championship cause but it was the personal highlight of a season in which Slack, who died tragically young in 1989, was Middlesex's leading Championship run-scorer with 1,618 at 47.59 and was picked for England's tour of the Caribbean.

Slack was a key member of the side by this point but this was the season when the understudies took centre stage. Three players (captain Mike Gatting, vice-captain John Emburey and wicketkeeper Paul Downton) played in all six Ashes Tests, Phil Edmonds played five and Norman Cowans one. Wisden had asked: "Are the reserves adequate?" The answer was unequivocal. "All the younger players filled in really well," says Emburey. "We went from one side to developing another."

All-rounder Graham Rose, 21, took 6 for 41 on his first-class debut at Worcester and Middlesex, thanks to a Roland Butcher century, won by three wickets. Experience told too, with Neil Williams returning to form towards the end of the season and Wayne Daniel, in his benefit year, bowling faster than for many years off a shortened run. He finished with a career-high 79 wickets.

The title was sealed in the final match at Edgbaston, a victory by an innings and 74 runs in which no Middlesex batsmen made a century or took five wickets.

John Stern

SEASON OF SUCCESS: 1990

HAYNES MAKES HAY

The Year of the Bat and the year of Desmond Haynes. Pitches were friendlier, the balls had reduced seams and Middlesex's West Indies opener, in his second year with the county, made merry. He scored 2,035 Championship runs, twice making a hundred before lunch, and was the competition sponsor's player of the year.

Middlesex, with Mike Gatting and John Emburey available for the whole season because of rebel-tour bans, won ten games and lost only at Derby on a pitch that would cause the home side to be docked 25 points. They resisted a late-season surge from Essex and took the title with an innings victory in their final match at Hove, Simon Hughes taking the crucial wicket on the last afternoon.

The season was notable for the growing maturity of a number younger players including Mike Roseberry, Mark Ramprakash (who played in all 22 matches), Angus Fraser and Phil Tufnell, who was the leading wicket-taker with 65. Chas Taylor, in only his second match, took 5 for 33 to secure a thrilling victory at Headingley. **JS**

SEASON OF SUCCESS: 1993

GREATER THAN THE SUM OF THEIR PARTS

An unexpected title, in the Championship's first full four-day programme, was delivered with 11 victories and defeat only in the final game but with no batsman making 1,000 Championship runs. "It was very much a team effort," reported *Wisden* before complaining about the average age (31) of the 11 players who had appeared in 13 or more matches.

In the club's annual review, David Kendix explained: "Eight of the 11 victories were achieved after losing the toss and being made to field first. Thereafter these matches followed a similar patter. In six of them, Middlesex were no more than 30 runs ahead on first innings, yet turned the game through bowling out their opponents cheaply second time around." John Emburey and Phil Tufnell (below) took 55 of these 80 wickets between them.

The most remarkable of these occurred halfway through the season at Cardiff. Glamorgan, who were joint top, made 562 for 3 declared with Adrian Dale and Viv Richards both making unbeaten double-centuries and putting on 425 for the fourth wicket. Middlesex, who went seven hours without a wicket, saved the follow-on and wanted to set up a game.

"We offered to declare behind but negotiations had broken down," says John Carr. Middlesex batted on and were all out for 584, thanks to centuries by Emburey and Mike Gatting who added 262 for the third wicket.

Only two sessions remained but this was to be no bore draw. "It was the most extraordinary game of cricket," says Carr, who took a simple, but very memorable, catch at short leg. Glamorgan were 62 for 3, all taken by Tufnell. "Viv Richards came out to bat with his usual positive body language," Carr remembers. "Viv always liked to make the bowler wait," says Tufnell. "So I stopped halfway through my run-up to move my field which was a bit brave of me! I could see that annoyed him."

Carr continues: "Tuffers got one to turn and bounce first ball and it just lobbed to me. He went wild with enthusiasm and celebrated very vigorously." Tufnell went on to take career-best figures of 8 for 29, Glamorgan were bowled out for 109 and Middlesex won by ten wickets to go 30 points clear at the top.

"At the end of the game Viv came into our dressing room looking rather solemn, looking out for Philip," says Carr. "Desi was winding me up, saying Viv wouldn't be happy," says Tufnell, who, according to Carr, was by now "cowering". Tufnell says: "Viv came up to me, put his hand out and just said, 'Well bowled young man'." My head was growing. That was the first time an opposition player – one of the greatest in the world – had taken time to come up to me and say 'well bowled'."

The title was won by the end of August following victory over defending champions Essex at Colchester and Northamptonshire's failure to beat Leicestershire. It is Middlesex's most recent County Championship title. **JS**

Made in Melbourne:
Albert Trott (left) and
Frank Tarrant

PROFILE BY MARCUS WILLIAMS

TRIUMPH AND TRAGEDY

Long before overseas players were an accepted part of the county game Middlesex
had two outstanding Australian all-rounders

Middlesex have been handsomely served in modern times by overseas players such as Wayne Daniel, Desmond Haynes, Justin Langer, Chris Rogers and Vintcent van der Bijl, but even their achievements were outdone by two Australians of a much earlier era, Albert Trott and Frank Tarrant. They shone in the summers before the First World War with a mass of runs and wickets – not to mention two feats that remain unparalleled to this day – but their lives after cricket progressed in starkly contrasting fashion.

Trott was first on the scene, becoming a Middlesex regular in 1898; Tarrant followed in 1905. Both had been on the Lord's groundstaff, playing for MCC and other invitation sides in England, but they had to serve a two-year qualifying period before they could appear in competitive matches as there were no instant registrations for overseas players until 1968.

Born in Melbourne, Trott sprang to prominence at the age of 21 with his outstanding performances against the touring English side led by another Middlesex stalwart, AE Stoddart, in 1894-95. He scored 331 runs in nine innings and took 19 wickets, topped by 38 and 72, both not out, and 8 for 43 in his debut Test at Adelaide. When Trott was surprisingly not selected for the 1896 tour to England, he came to England of his own accord and was taken on at Lord's.

Tarrant was also from Melbourne, where he was for a time a ground bowler earning 30 shillings a week, and little was known about him when he joined the Lord's staff in 1903 aged 22. Tarrant's abilities were soon recognised and in that first season he played for the Players against the Gentlemen at Scarborough, where he appeared alongside Trott as well as in opposition to two other Middlesex men in Plum Warner and Bernard Bosanquet (the inventor of the googly or Bosie as it used to be known in Australia).

Trott, too, had made an immediate impact when he first turned out for Middlesex in 1898. A hand injury kept him out of the early games but by August he and JT Hearne were in such irresistible form with the ball that the county won eight matches out of nine in August. Trott's final tally was 102 wickets in 14 matches as well as 389 runs.

The next two seasons saw Trott at the peak of his powers. In first-class matches in 1899 he scored 1,175 runs and took 239 wickets, and in 1900 his figures were 1,337 runs and 211 wickets, including all ten in Somerset's first innings at Taunton. With his bowling, powerful hitting and superb fielding he became a favourite of the Lord's crowd. The strength of his bowling lay in its varieties and changes of pace; he seldom bowled two balls alike and could produce a devastatingly fast yorker.

In May 1899 at Lord's Trott made 164, his highest first-class score, off a Yorkshire attack containing Rhodes, Haigh, Hirst and Jackson, the last 137 runs coming in an hour and a half. One drive hit the pavilion rails with such force that it rebounded to mid-on. On July 31 he produced the feat for which he will forever be remembered: he is the only batsman to have hit a ball over the present Lord's pavilion. The great strike was made off Monty Noble's bowling when Trott was playing for MCC against the Australians. He had played himself in carefully, but then unleashed one drive on to the top deck of the pavilion followed by an even bigger one which went over the top and landed in a garden behind.

Warner wrote later that the record hit ruined Trott's batting as "ever afterwards he went around armed with a 3lb club trying to carry pavilions", and it is true that he never reached 1,000 runs in a season after 1900.

He took 176 wickets in 1901 and passed 100 in the next three seasons, including Middlesex's Championship-winning year of 1903, but his form with the bat showed a steady decline as eventually did his bowling. Part of the problem was that Trott, who liked his beer, had put on weight and could no longer produce his threatening

" **Trott shot himself at his digs in Willesden Green, having written his will on the back of a laundry ticket**

quicker ball. He did, however, earn another place in the record books in 1907 when he cut short his own benefit match against Somerset with his second unique achievement: two hat-tricks – the first actually four wickets in four balls – in the same innings.

Tarrant, meanwhile, had established himself in the Middlesex eleven. When he qualified for Middlesex in 1905, he had already built up a reputation, and two years later he was rated the best all-round cricketer in England. In eight consecutive seasons he completed the double of 1,000 runs and 100 wickets. In 1907 his figures were 1,552 runs and 183 wickets, and in 1911 he scored 2,030 runs and took 111 wickets.

He was a dynamic cricketer, who appeared to enjoy every moment of a game whether batting, bowling or fielding. At the wicket he was sometimes cautious, but he was a good cutter and developed his leg-side strokes. He bowled left-arm, varying his pace from slow to medium, and could run through a side on a damaged pitch. Not without justification has he been described as perhaps the best player never to have won a Test cap; his time in England, and a short spell back home in 1907-08, ruled him out of playing for either country. Seventeen appearances for the Players against the Gentlemen were the height of his representative cricket.

Altogether in England he scored 15,903 runs with an average of nearly 36, and captured 1,335 wickets for less than 18 runs apiece; his figures for Middlesex were 12,169 (average 38.02) and 1,005 (17.43, the lowest figure by any bowler to have taken more than 1,000 wickets for the county). Five times Tarrant took nine wickets in an innings, he achieved five hat-tricks and he made 33 hundreds (26 for Middlesex) of which four were doubles, including 250 not out when Middlesex, after being put in, scored 464 for 1 declared and beat Essex by an innings at Leyton in May 1914.

Two months after that remarkable match Tarrant's countryman Trott was dead. He had played his last match for Middlesex in 1910, and the following season his first-class career of 10,696 runs and 1,674 wickets (946 for Middlesex) concluded on a sad note with a pair for MCC against Cambridge University at Lord's. A far greater tragedy, however, was to follow.

After retiring as a player he joined the first-class umpires list, but by May 1914 his health was so poor – he suffered from oedema – that he had to give up. On July 30, with no hope of recovery, he shot himself at his digs in Willesden Green, aged 41. He had written his will on the back of a laundry ticket, leaving his wardrobe and £4 to his landlady.

Tarrant's later years could hardly have been more different. After the First World War he returned home and played with some success for Victoria in 1924-25. He also earned a considerable income from buying and selling racehorses in Australia and India, where he numbered princes among his friends and turned out for various sides.

Frank was employed as cricket coach and adviser first to the Maharajah of Cooch-Behar and then to the Maharajah of Patiala, under whose auspices he took an Australian team to India in the winter of 1935-36. He played his last first-class match, at the age of 56, opening the bowling with Harold Larwood and still good enough to score 78 in the first innings, for the Europeans against the Hindus in the final of the Bombay Quadrangular tournament in December 1936. He died back in Melbourne in January 1951. ●

ALBERT EDWIN TROTT
Born: February 6, 1873, Melbourne
Died: July 30, 1914, Willesden Green
Right-hand batsman, right-arm medium-pace bowler

- 3 Tests for Australia 1894-95
- Took 8 for 43 on Test debut for Australia v England at Adelaide 1894-95 – the best Test bowling figures on debut
- 2 Tests for England 1898-99
- 6,253 first-class runs (10,696 overall) for Middlesex at 20.23, 1898–1910
- 946 first-class wickets (1,674 overall) for Middlesex including 71 5-fors and 23 10-wicket matches
- 1,674 first-class wickets overall
- Took all ten wickets (10 for 42) for Middlesex v Somerset 1900
- Championship title 1903
- Took two hat-tricks in second innings of Middlesex v Somerset (his own benefit match) at Lord's 1907
- Wisden Cricketer of the Year 1899
- Middlesex benefit 1907

FRANK ALFRED TARRANT
Born: December 11, 1880, Melbourne
Died: January 29, 1951, Melbourne
Right-hand batsman, left-arm slow-medium bowler

- 12,169 first-class runs for Middlesex (17,952 overall) at 38.02 1904–14, best 250*
- One of nine bowlers to take more than 1,000 first-class wickets for Middlesex (1,005); 1,512 first-class wickets overall
- Did the double of 1,000 runs and 100 wickets in eight consecutive seasons
- Has lowest bowling average of the nine bowlers to have taken 1,000 or more first-class wickets for Middlesex
- Most hat-tricks (4) for Middlesex
- Wisden Cricketer of the Year 1908
- Middlesex benefit 1914

JACKS OF ALL TRADES

For almost half a century a pair of distant cousins, the **Hearnes**, who also bore the same first name, were central to the Middlesex cause with bat and ball

Middlesex have a long tradition of families who have played large parts in the county's history, starting with the Walker brothers and continuing through the Fords, Studds, Manns and Comptons to name only a few. In terms of service, however, none of these can match the Hearnes, JT (John Thomas) and JW (John William) both known as Jack, who between 1888 and 1936 – their careers overlapping for a few seasons before the First World War – made a total of 918 appearances for the county and stand high in their all-time record lists.

They were actually distant cousins (second, once removed), and JT's part of the family had a strong cricketing pedigree. He was a nephew of Tom and George Hearne, both of whom played for Buckinghamshire and Middlesex in the 1860s and 1870s, and his brothers, Herbert and Walter, as well as cousins George G., Frank and Alec Hearne, all played as professionals for Kent. Frank emigrated to South Africa and one of his sons later won Test caps for that country.

JT, who was born in Buckinghamshire at Chalfont St Giles, and came to Middlesex on the initiative of the captain, AJ Webbe, who had spotted his potential. He was employed for most of his career as a professional bowler by MCC, which meant bowling in matches for the club as well as being made available to play for Middlesex and later England. He made a single appearance for the county against the Australians in 1888 at the age of 21, but came to the fore in 1890 when he took six Nottinghamshire wickets, including the great Arthur Shrewsbury, for 62 on his

Championship debut and the county had found the front-line bowler they had lacked for many years. The following summer he took 14 for 65 against Yorkshire, at Lord's, and went on to bag 129 wickets at an average of 11.30 in all first-class matches to finish top of the national list (a placing he repeated in 1910). He never looked back.

> ❝ Wisden predicted a great future for JW: 'there is no reason why he should not develop into the best batsman in England'

In 1893 he took 212 wickets and in 1896, his best season, his tally rose to 257 wickets at 14.72 each. He played in all three Tests, taking 15 wickets at 14.1 each, ten of them coming in the final match at The Oval, at a cost of only 60, when England secured the series. He had been in even more destructive form earlier in the tour: playing for MCC at Lord's he took 4 for 4 as the Australians were bowled out for 18 and then claimed all nine wickets that fell – one player was absent – for 73.

He went on the 1897-98 tour to Australia and his nine wickets for 141 in the first Test at Sydney were a major factor in England's only win before Australia won the remaining four matches. He played in three of the Ashes Tests in 1899 and at Headingley claimed what remains the only hat-trick by

JOHN THOMAS HEARNE
Born: May 3, 1867, Chalfont St Giles
Died: April 17, 1944, Chalfont St Giles
Right-arm medium-pace bowler, right-hand batsman

- Second in all-time list of Middlesex first-class wicket-takers behind
  Fred Titmus
- 2,093 first-class wickets (3,061 overall) for Middlesex at 18.23
  1888–1923
- Wisden Cricketer of the Year 1892
- 49 wickets at 22.08 in 12 Tests
- 100 or more wickets in eight successive seasons 1891–98 (best 145 in 1893)
- Leading wicket-taker with 76 at 17.40 in Championship-winning
  1903 season

JOHN WILLIAM HEARNE
Born: February 11, 1891, Uxbridge
Died: September 14, 1965, West Drayton
Right-hand batsman, right-arm leg-spin bowler

- 27,612 first-class runs (37,252 overall) at 41.15 for Middlesex 1909–36
- Third-highest run-scorer for the county
- 71 hundreds is third-most for the county
- Top score of 285* v Essex at Leyton in 1929 is third highest for Middlesex
- 806 runs at 26.00 in 24 Tests
- Third most first-class wickets for Middlesex (1,438)
- Championship titles 1920 (most wickets 119), 1921
- Wisden Cricketer of the Year 1912
- Middlesex benefit 1925, 1932

an England bowler against Australia in a Test in this country. His victims were three of the opposition's best batsmen, Clem Hill, Sid Gregory and Monty Noble. He achieved three other hat-tricks in his career, all for Middlesex, including four in five balls against Essex at Lord's in 1902, and, as with his county debut, he went out with a bang: on his last Middlesex appearance at Lord's in 1914 he took 7 for 65 and 2 for 3 against Kent, one of his final victims being Frank Woolley. He even came out of retirement for one last hurrah at the age of 56 when a strong Middlesex XI travelled to Edinburgh for a first-class friendly match against Scotland in 1923. He rolled back the years with six wickets in the match, a useful 20 runs and a nonchalant catch.

> ❝ JT bowled medium pace with a high action, a good off-cutter and variations of pace which made him challenging on good wickets and devastating on bad ones

JT took a hundred wickets in a season 15 times (ten for Middlesex), passing 200 three times, with a best of 257 in 1896. His career total of 3,061 places him fourth on the all-time list behind the spinners Rhodes, Freeman and Parker, and for Middlesex his 2,093 has been surpassed only by Fred Titmus's 2,361. He bowled medium pace with a high action, a good off-cutter and variations of pace which made him challenging on good wickets and devastating on bad ones. He was a good fielder, specialising close to the wicket, but as a tailender never achieved much with the bat, his best score for Middlesex in more than 600 innings being 56 not out.

By then he was a member of the Middlesex committee, having been elected in 1920, a rare honour for a professional in those days. He subsequently coached the Oxford University team and was popular with generations of undergraduates for the modesty and kindness that he showed throughout his life. 'Old Jack' died back home in Chalfont in 1944.

'Young Jack' (JW), who was born in Uxbridge, joined the Lord's staff as a ground boy in 1906 when he was 15; his duties included selling scorecards, cleaning the ground

and helping to push the heavy roller. He made his debut for Middlesex three years later with moderate success, but stepped into the limelight the following season when he took seven wickets for no runs in 25 balls against Essex at Lord's and made hundreds against Somerset and Sussex. From then until 1935 he was a fixture in the county side.

He started out as a leg spinner with great powers of spin and a well-disguised googly – and the shortest of run-ups – but a wrist injury caused him to favour the off break after the First World War. He ended his career with a total of 1,839 wickets at 24.42, of which 1,438 were for Middlesex. If you add to those his 37,252 runs at 40.98, including 96 centuries (27,612 and 71 for Middlesex), compiled in a stylish and unhurried style, you have figures that set him among the front rank of all-rounders. He achieved the double five times, his best season being Middlesex's Championship-winning year of 1920 when he scored 2,148 runs and took 148 wickets in all matches.

In 19 seasons he scored more than 1,000 runs, four times passing 2,000, and he made 11 double-centuries, his highest being 285 not out against Essex at Leyton in 1929. Always immaculately turned out, he shared many big partnerships with his great friend Patsy Hendren, in a famous combination for Middlesex that foreshadowed that of Compton and Edrich in later years. His largest stand with Hendren was 375 for the third wicket against Hampshire at Southampton in 1923, when the first four batsmen all scored hundreds and Middlesex made their record total of 642 for three declared; the pair made 325 against the same opponents at Lord's four years earlier. Hearne also took part in a stand of 380 with Frank Tarrant against Lancashire at Lord's in 1914.

He played in 24 Tests for England either side of the First World War, making a wonderful start but never again touching the heights. He went on the tour to Australia in 1911-12 led by Plum Warner, his county captain, who championed his cause when some Middlesex committee members considered him too young, at the age of 20, for such an arduous trip; the team were away for the best part of six months in those days. Ironically it was Warner himself who was taken ill on that trip and missed the entire Test series, which produced one of England's greatest triumphs down under, whereas Hearne made a fine impression.

After scoring 76 and 43 in the first Test at Sydney he

followed with a chanceless 114 at Melbourne to become the youngest England player to score a hundred against Australia, and he held the record until it was beaten by Denis Compton in 1938. Hearne's batting fell away in the rest of the series despite England's 4-1 victory, but *Wisden's* summary predicted a great future for him: "there is no reason why he should not develop into the best batsman in England."

Sadly the promise never came to fruition in the international game. He played with mixed success in the rain-ruined Triangular Tournament of 1912 and on the 1913-14 tour of South Africa where he was afflicted by flu. Illness intervened again in Australia during 1920-21, when he started in fine form but was struck down on the opening day of the second Test and did not reappear on the tour. He made occasional appearances thereafter, including the next visit to Australia, but his England career ended in the washed out match against Australia at Trent Bridge in 1926. In 24 Tests his full record was 806 runs (average 26.00) and 30 wickets (48.73).

Despite his health problems, and an assumed susceptibility to injury, Hearne did not flinch from powerful hits. At Lord's in 1928, for instance, when Learie Constantine inspired a sensational three-wicket victory for the West Indians over Middlesex, Hearne instinctively grabbed at a ferocious return from Constantine and the resulting broken hand put him out of cricket for the last 12 weeks of the season. It was a particular blow as he was averaging over 70 at the time, form that he recaptured on occasions – notably in 1932 when, at the age of 41, he scored 2,151 runs including six centuries.

Always immensely popular, with his quiet manner and subtle sense of humour, Hearne went into coaching after retirement, first at King's College School, Wimbledon, and then at Lord's where aspiring Middlesex players came under his wing. In 1949 he was one of 26 former professional players honoured with life membership by MCC. Like his cousin, JT, he was an unassuming man, always helpful and encouraging to others, and was much mourned when he died in September 1965 at West Drayton. ●

ANOTHER HEARNE WHO HAD A MUCH BRIEFER CAREER

Another member of the Hearne clan, Thomas John, holds an unenviable record which makes him the subject of arcane cricketing quizzes: he was selected for only one first-class match in his career but, although it consisted of four innings, he never managed to take the field.

How did this happen? He had been called up as a late replacement for his cousin, JT, by Middlesex for a match against the Gentlemen of Philadelphia at Lord's on July 20, 1908, but the game was played on such a treacherous pitch that it lasted only 91.3 overs and finished in a day. Hearne arrived late in the afternoon, by when Middlesex were into their second innings and he was not required to bat, although he would have done if required. He did play once for Middlesex Second XI the following season and after the First World War for Berkshire in the Minor Counties Championship but never had another opportunity on the first-class stage.

Philadelphians 58 (Tarrant 5-19, Trott 5-31) and 55 (Tarrant 5-27, Trott 4-28); Middlesex 92 (King 4-19) and 24-3.

PROFILE BY MARCUS WILLIAMS

AS GOOD AS ANYONE

Patsy Hendren was Middlesex's peerless run machine with humour and popularity to match

Patsy Hendren, a Middlesex favourite between the First and Second World Wars, is not always quoted in the same breath as the game's immortals, but his first-class career statistics place him very high indeed in the cricketing panoply: 170 centuries, second only to Hobbs; 57,611 runs, third only to Hobbs and Woolley; 1,000 runs or more in a season 25 times, beaten only by Grace, Woolley, Cowdrey, Mead, Boycott and Hobbs; exceeding 3,000 three times, equalled only by Sutcliffe and Hammond, and 2,000 12 times. He was also an outstanding fielder, which first brought him to prominence, and more than 750 catches were pouched in his safe hands.

Figures alone tell little of the man. The universal image of Patsy – it is hard to imagine anyone calling him by his given names, Elias Henry – is of a perky, genial character, an entertainer who loved to play cricket and was the darling of the Lord's crowd in the inter-war years as Compton and Edrich were to be afterwards. The tremendous ovation he received in his final match there, against Surrey in 1937, was proof.

Aged 48, he fittingly made a hundred in the first innings and the 17,000 crowd rose to their feet and stopped play for several minutes to sing "For he's a jolly good fellow". Despite the anti-climax of a duck in the second innings he was applauded to and from the wicket by players and supporters alike. He was immensely popular with his fellow players and would have the dressing room in uproar with his mimicry and wit. Jack Hobbs called him "the life and soul of the party" not to mention "as good a player as anyone".

Born of Irish extraction at Turnham Green in 1889, Hendren, like many, graduated to Middlesex via the Lord's

groundstaff. He prided himself that he was never coached and modelled his play on the Lancastrian, Johnny Tyldesley, another compact figure who excelled in the speed of his footwork. Square and muscular, Hendren crouched slightly at the wicket, which made him appear smaller than he actually was. As with all the great batsmen, he possessed a sound and orthodox defence, but his strength and ability made him a master of all the strokes except the late cut. He excelled in the hook and square drive, and late in his career developed a lofted drive to mid-wicket, akin to the modern slog-sweep. Above all, he was never dull to watch and would doubtless have excelled in limited-overs cricket if it had been played in his day.

Hendren made his debut for Middlesex (though *Wisden* and the county's history credit the appearance to his brother, Denis) in the infamous 1907 match in which Archie MacLaren, the Lancashire captain, refused to go on beyond the second day because he claimed the pitch had been deliberately damaged by spectators following a rumpus which followed play being called off after a long rain delay. Hendren wrote many years later that the ferrule of an umbrella had been stuck into the pitch, other reports said it was a heel mark; however slight the damage it was too much for the autocratic MacLaren.

Hendren's early years in the side were not blessed with great success and though he was awarded his cap in 1909 after scoring 71 against a Yorkshire attack containing Hirst, Haigh and Rhodes – going down on one knee to have the cap placed on his head by his captain, Plum Warner – it was after the First World War that he really established himself as a key member of the side. He had already made his mark as a footballer with

ELIAS HENRY HENDREN
Born: February 5, 1889, Turnham Green
Died: October 4, 1962, Tooting Bec
Right-hand batsman, right-arm slow bowler

- Most first-class runs for Middlesex (40,302 at 49.81) 1907–37 and 57,611 overall
- Most hundreds for Middlesex (119) and 170 overall
- 3,525 runs in 51 Tests at 47.63
- Passed 2,000 runs in a season 14 times
- Wisden Cricketer of the Year 1920
- Middlesex benefit 1923, 1931, 1935 (testimonial)

MOST FIRST-CLASS RUNS FOR MIDDLESEX

40,302	EH Hendren
28,411	MW Gatting
27,612	JW Hearne
27,088	JDB Robertson
25,738	WJ Edrich

MOST FIRST-CLASS CENTURIES FOR MIDDLESEX

119	EH Hendren
77	MW Gatting
71	JW Hearne
67	DCS Compton
62	WJ Edrich

MOST FIRST-CLASS RUNS IN A SEASON FOR MIDDLESEX

2,669	EH Hendren	1923
2,650	WJ Edrich	1947
2,623	EH Hendren	1928
2,622	JDB Robertson	1951
2,514	EH Hendren	1933

Brentford, being chosen for England in a Victory international against Wales.

His performances in 1919 brought recognition as one of *Wisden*'s Five Cricketers of the Year and, after heading the national averages in Middlesex's Championship-winning summer of 1920, he was selected for the winter tour of Australia. Though he was, by some distance, the leading run-maker in all matches, he performed only moderately in the Tests, all of which England lost. He was to go twice more to Australia, each time enjoying greater success outside the Test matches, although on his last visit, in 1928-29, he made a superb 169 in the opening match of the rubber at Brisbane, showing great composure at a crucial stage and then unfolding a fine array of strokes to set England on the way to victory by 675 runs and a 4-1 win in the series.

Packing them in: Patsy Hendren batting at Canterbury in 1923 in a seven-wicket victory for Middlesex during which he passed 13,000 career runs

"Jack Hobbs called him 'the life and soul of the party'

Hendren enjoyed other successes overseas, not least the 1929-30 tour to the West Indies, when, passing his 41st birthday, he revelled in the hard pitches to the extent of four unbeaten double centuries – including 205 in the second Test at Port of Spain – and two centuries, and altogether scored 1,765 runs at an average of 135.76. The achievements were all the more worthy because, in several of the matches, he faced Constantine bowling at his fastest with a bodyline field. The memories were not lost on Hendren, for, when he faced Constantine and Martindale at Lord's in 1933, he wore a protective cap designed by his wife Minnie. It had three peaks, the extra two covering his ears and temples, and was lined with sponge rubber. It was another Middlesex giant, Mike Brearley, who was the next to sport similar headgear before helmets became standard issue for batsmen.

Though Hendren's record in home Tests was inconsistent, it had its highlights. He hit successive hundreds against South Africa in 1924 and then 127 not out against Australia at Lord's in 1926, the only Test century by a Middlesex batsman on his home ground against Australia until Andrew Strauss in 2009 and one which gave him, a former scorecard seller, the utmost pride. When recalled to the colours against Australia eight years later he helped England to avoid the follow-on with 79

at Trent Bridge and then scored 132 at Old Trafford in the penultimate of his 51 Tests.

For almost two decades he scored prodigiously for Middlesex, frequently heading the averages, run aggregates and total of centuries, and he remains – almost certainly for all time given that far less first-class cricket is now played – the county's record-holder with 40,302 runs (average 49.81), 119 centuries, 1,000 runs in a season 20 times, and 561 catches. Only Fred Titmus, with 642 appearances to Hendren's 581, surpasses him for longevity in the county side and only Jack Robertson's 331 not out against Worcestershire in 1949 beats Hendren's 301 not out against the same opponents in 1933.

Hendren formed a famous middle-order partnership with his friend, JW Hearne, and they still hold the record for the county's fourth wicket, 325 against Hampshire at Lord's in 1919. Hendren also has the seventh-wicket record of 271 with Frank Mann against Nottinghamshire at Trent Bridge in 1925.

After retirement from county cricket Hendren went on to coach at Harrow School (his second year in charge saw the first win over Eton for 31 years) and Sussex, and was made an honorary life member of MCC in 1949. He was Middlesex scorer from 1952 to 1960, as well as a member of the committee until his health failed before his death in October 1962. Sir Neville Cardus provided an appropriate epitaph: "His smile, on the field, as well as off it, is so wide that I often expected he would one day be given out 'Smile before wicket.'" ●

UNITED AND SUSTAINABLE

Katie Berry explains how the management of the recreational game in Middlesex and beyond has developed since the formation of the ECB in 1997

From 1968 cricket in this country was run by the Test and County Cricket Board (professional game) and National Cricket Association (recreational cricket) under the auspices of the (MCC) Cricket Council. Under the NCA's banner, counties were encouraged to set up county cricket associations to bring together all aspects of the recreational game in their areas. Middlesex chose the title Middlesex Cricket Union (MCU) to be shown as an inclusive, united body, which formed in 1970.

On January 1, 1997 the England and Wales Cricket Board (ECB) was launched combining the roles of the TCCB, NCA and Cricket Council forming the national governing body for cricket. The concept of the ECB was discussed in late 1995 and at a county level it was envisaged that a county board should be formed, mirroring the ECB, to bring together the professional and recreational game in each county. This concept went for both first-class and minor counties, originally forming 38 county boards.

The Middlesex Cricket Board's formation process was comprehensive, taking around 15 months and including widespread consultation with all the game's stakeholders. The process was led by the then MCU chairman David Holland and Middlesex player John Carr.

In December 1996 two annual general meetings were held: one to wind up the MCU and agree to transfer its assets to the MCB, and then the inaugural AGM of MCB to confirm its constitution and elect its officers and committee. This included four officers from the county club, including chairman Alan Moss, who became chairman of the board, and David Green as the chair of youth and coaching. MCU supplied the honorary secretary (Henry Painton) and treasurer (Michael Browne), plus the chairmen of committees for cricket (Terence Woram), publicity (Ken Johnston) and facilities (Graham Hall). There was also a representative from schools cricket (John Stacey).

The key driver of the county boards at the time was the availability of funds through the Cricket Foundation to support development work which had never previously existed. Thus was born the concept of development plans, annual reports, and submissions to the Cricket Foundation.

Lord Maclaurin's *Raising the Standard* was the first published ECB plan in 1997, which sparked discussion about the future of county second XI and minor counties cricket and led to the formation of premier leagues for club cricket. Also at that time, many more funding streams became available because of the lottery and Sport England contributions, so facilities issues became a key focal point. Middlesex CCC was a generous provider for our facilities fund, which supported projects outside the scope of other grant-making bodies. The MCB continues to build on these themes today, with funding, facilities and coaching remaining as key priorities for the board.

The new 'outcome approach' to cricket development introduced for the 2013–17 whole sport plan period will allow the MCB greater flexibility to offer local opportunities to play, watch and follow the game for all communities in Middlesex. It will see the county club, MCB, Middlesex Cricket Trust and the respective leagues work together via an integrated network, creating resource efficiencies and operational effectiveness. The board will allocate future resources based on the needs of our customers and will support clubs via the National Club Strategy to ensure a sustainable future for the game in Middlesex. ●

Katie Berry is the Middlesex Cricket Board's director of development

EVERYBODY'S HEROES

Barry Norman on his childhood idols, Denis Compton and Bill Edrich, Middlesex legends whom he would later come to know and even share a cricket field with

It's the boyhood heroes who remain sharpest in the memory and for me the mention of Middlesex cricket will always conjure up the names of Bill Edrich and Denis Compton. Back in that *annus mirabilis* of 1947 when Denis scored a record-breaking 3,816 runs and Bill was not far behind with 3,539, they were everybody's heroes.

Bill was the one I saw first, at Lord's in August 1945, in a Victory Test against the Australian Services. The opposition that day included a handy and decidedly quick young bowler called Keith Miller but Bill, small, bare-headed and belligerent, laid confidently into him and his colleagues to score 73 not out.

I next saw him, again at Lord's, in 1947. Middlesex versus Warwickshire and again he was up against a tall and decidedly sharp fast bowler – the New Zealander Tom Pritchard. Bill, utterly fearless, skipped down the wicket and drove him back over his head into the pavilion. What was there not to admire in this – a six-stone weakling kicking sand into the face of the bully?

Denis, though, was something else again – the Brylcreem boy, so handsome as to be catnip to women wherever he went, a professional playing his cricket like an old-time amateur of independent means as if it wasn't work at all but simply sheer pleasure. And that pleasure transmitted itself to the crowd so that we, the onlookers, derived almost as much joy from a Compton innings as he obviously did.

I only met Bill once when I was invited to play in a charity match under his captaincy. He asked me if I bowled; I said I did and he threw me the ball. What I bowled purported to be leg-breaks. These left the batsmen deeply unimpressed as they

showed in the pitiless way batsmen will. After a while Bill took me off. "I think you're looking tired," he said. I had bowled three overs but it was kind of him to spare me further humiliation.

My first meeting with Denis was at a Saints and Sinners dinner at the Savoy Hotel in London. I was there, naturally, as a Saint, Denis, just as naturally, as a Sinner; his severest critic would never have accused him of being a Saint.

At the end of the evening those left on his table joined the people remaining on ours and Denis chose to sit next to me. I was overwhelmed. He could have sat next to anybody but he picked me. Wow!

And much better still it turned out that we had a sort of mutual admiration society going on (the admiration far greater, surely, on my side than his). He, it transpired, was a movie buff who enjoyed my TV programme and wanted to talk about the film stars I had met, while all I wanted to talk about was cricket.

Finally I got my chance and asked him something that had perplexed me for years: namely was it true that at Trent Bridge in 1938 he, aged 20 and playing in his first Ashes Test, had to be woken up to be told it was his turn to bat? He said it was; I said I couldn't believe it; he said: "Well, it was a hot day, Len Hutton had got a few and so had Joe Hardstaff and I just sort of nodded off."

Of course, when he'd rubbed the sleep from his eyed he scored 102 before being caught on the boundary. He returned to the pavilion to a standing ovation, expecting much the same in the England dressing room only to be met at the door by his

Entertainment guaranteed: Bill Edrich (left) and Denis Compton stride to the crease against Sussex at Lord's in 1947. Both made first-innings hundreds in a third-wicket stand of 223 and Middlesex won by ten wickets

DENIS CHARLES SCOTT COMPTON

Born: May 23, 1918, Hendon
Died: April 23, 1997, Windsor
Right-hand batsman, slow left-arm chinaman bowler

- 21,781 first-class runs (38,942 overall) for Middlesex at 49.95 1936–58, 67 hundreds
- 5,807 runs in 78 Tests; one of eight England batsmen to average over 50 in Tests (minimum 20 innings)
- His 18 hundreds in 1947 is a record for a first-class season
- Passed 2,000 runs in a season six times (best 3,816 in 1947)
- 477 first-class wickets at 29.61 for Middlesex
- Middlesex benefit 1949
- Middlesex captain 1951–52
- Middlesex cap 1936
- Wisden Cricketer of the Year 1939
- Football for England (war-time international) and Arsenal
- Awarded CBE 1958

WILLIAM JOHN EDRICH

Born: March 26, 1916, Lingwood, Norfolk
Died: April 24 1986, Chesham, Buckinghamshire
Right-hand batsman, right-arm fast-medium/off-spin bowler

- 25,738 first-class runs (36,965 overall) at 43.40 for Middlesex 1937–58
- 2,440 runs at 40.00 in 39 Tests
- Passed 2,000 runs in a season nine times (best 3,539 in 1947)
- 328 first-class wickets for Middlesex
- Also played four one-day (List A) matches for Norfolk 1965–70
- Middlesex cap 1937
- Wisden Cricketer of the Year 1940
- Middlesex captain 1951–57

> **If you wanted someone to bat for your life Bill would be the better choice. But if you wanted someone to make your last hours on earth as enjoyable as possible it had to be Denis**

grim-faced skipper Walter Hammond saying: "Don't you ever again let me see you get out to a shot like that in a Test match."

But that was Denis. Like Kevin Pietersen, only without the ego and with a far, far greater sense of fun, he played the game his way. He had every shot in the book plus a few known only to himself.

At The Oval in 1947, for instance, for Middlesex the County Champions versus The Rest, he went down the wicket to Tom Goddard, the Gloucestershire off-spinner, who had taken 208 wickets that year, tripped over his own feet, fell flat on his face and swept the ball for four at the same time. Only Denis could have done that.

He and the less inventive but equally aggressive and fast-scoring Edrich were the perfect pair. In 1947 they racked up partnership after partnership and Middlesex always seemed to declare at about 420 for 6 at teatime on the first day.

If Denis had a flaw it was his judgement of a run. I believe it was Bill who first said that any call from Denis, be it "Yes", "No" or "Wait", was simply the opening of negotiations and he spoke only the truth.

I was at Lord's for the first day of Denis' brother Leslie's benefit match – Middlesex versus Sussex. The home team were going well and Denis was at the wicket when Leslie, the side's wicketkeeper-batsman, came out to join him. A benefit match and the beneficiary and his sibling batting together, what more could one ask?

Well, a lot more than one got, in fact. Within a couple of minutes Denis had run his brother out for a duck. "Yes – wait – no – yes – hang on!" Denis was rushing around pleading with everybody that it wasn't his fault while the Sussex fielders,

knowing it was, clutched their sides with mirth.

Many years later I asked Denis what Leslie had said as, in thunderous mood, he walked past him on the way back to the pavilion. "I can tell you exactly," he said. "What he said was 'If you don't score a hundred today, little brother, I'm going to f***** murder you.'" Inevitably Denis scored a hundred, a big one.

If you wanted one of those two, Edrich and Compton, to bat for your life Bill would probably be the better choice, though I wouldn't necessarily bank on it because earnest wicket- and life-saving defence was never his first choice. But if you wanted someone to make your last hours on earth as enjoyable as possible it had to be Denis.

In recent years (although not, alas, all that recent) Middlesex have gone on to greater glories under the captaincy of the two Mikes, Brearley and Gatting. But the 1947 side was rather special.

Along with Compton and Edrich it also included that consummate stylist Jack Robertson, than whom nobody since has made the late cut look so elegant. And one day at Lord's they opened the bowling against Kent with the right-arm fast medium of Laurie Gray and, at the other end, the left-arm spin of Jack Young.

CHELTENHAM CHALLENGE

The key match in Middlesex's 1947 Championship-winning campaign

Gloucestershire were four points clear of Middlesex at the top of the Championship when the two sides met in August at Cheltenham College. It was a match that, according to *Wisden*, "vied for chief interest among cricket followers with the fifth Test, which deprived Middlesex of the help of Denis Compton and Robertson."

A crowd of 14,500, a record for Cheltenham, watched the first day's play and saw 21 wickets fall, eight of them to the great Gloucestershire off-spinner, Tom Goddard, who arrested Middlesex's decent start with seven in the first innings and then another before the close after his own side had conceded a first-innings deficit of 27. Goddard finished with 15 in the match.

Nightwatchman Harry Sharp and the captain Walter Robins put on 70 in 50 minutes in Middlesex's second innings on

the second day but eight wickets fell for 38 runs, leaving Gloucestershire 169 to win.

Sharp, whose 46 was his highest first-class score, then turned his off-breaks to good use, breaking a third-wicket stand of 35 between Jack Crapp and William Neale, who was caught at short leg. He had George Emmett caught behind next ball.

The rest of the innings was cleaned up by the frontline spin of Jack Young and Jim Sims. Middlesex had usurped Gloucestershire at the top of the table and, with four matches of the season, left were heading for their first title since 1921 after finishing second five years running. "In all ways," *Wisden* said, "Middlesex provided the best illustration of the 'dynamic attitude' ideal of the MCC Select Committee."

At Cheltenham, August 16, 18, 1947. Middlesex won by 68 runs.
†Middlesex 180 (WJ Edrich 50; TWJ Goddard 7-70) and 141 (Goddard 8-86); Gloucestershire 153 (JM Sims 6-65, JA Young 4-55) and 100 (Young 5-27).

How often nowadays, save in highly exceptional circumstances, are you likely to see a spinner take the new ball on day one of a championship match?

But in that age of uncovered wickets Middlesex had tremendous faith in spin bowlers. Frequently the side would include four and on at least one occasion there were five: three leggies in the captain Walter Robins, Jim Sims and the gifted but tragically short-lived Ian Bedford, plus Jack Young and Denis's erratic but always interesting chinamen.

These days hardly any county picks more than one spinner and he is usually employed to bowl flat off-breaks, not in the hope of taking wickets but merely to keep one end quiet.

Cricket has developed hugely since that summer of 1947, especially in the fielding. Back then the elderly Sims, standing at mid-wicket, would watch the ball pass him with great interest, confident that someone younger would run round the boundary to pick it up. He couldn't get away with that now.

But nobody since has equalled – or ever will equal – the feats of Denis and Bill that year and no English batsman, with the possible exception of David Gower, has ever played with the sheer, unalloyed enjoyment of the peerless Denis Compton. ●

Barry Norman first presented the Film *programme on BBC television in 1972 before moving to Sky in 1998. He has been following Middlesex for more than 50 years*

1947

That year of peerless batting in numbers

LEADING FIRST-CLASS AVERAGES FOR 1947 SEASON

	M	Inns	NO	Runs	HS	Avge	100	50
DCS Compton	30	50	8	3816	246	90.85	18	12
(Middx, Eng, MCC, Players, South)								
WJ Edrich	30	52	8	3539	267*	80.43	12	15
(Middx, Eng, Gents, South)								
JDB Robertson	32	57	4	2760	229	52.07	12	6
(Middx, Eng, MCC, Gents, Players, South)								

AND IN MATCHES ONLY FOR MIDDLESEX

	M	Inns	NO	Runs	HS	Avge	100	50
WJ Edrich	22	38	7	2650	267*	85.48	10	9
DCS Compton	19	31	7	2467	246	102.79	13	5
JDB Robertson	26	45	3	2328	229	55.42	11	4

MIDDLESEX'S LEADING BOWLERS IN 1947

	Wkts	Best	Avge	5wi	10wm
JA Young	139	7-46	16.54	10	1
(left-arm orthodox spin)					
JM Sims	120	6-65	25.36	5	1
(right-arm off-spin)					
LH Gray	92	7-69	22.46	3	0
(right-arm fast-medium)					
DCS Compton	63	6-78	25.22	4	1
(left-arm chinamen)					
WJ Edrich	50	6-28	21.90	3	1
(right-arm fast-medium)					

Museum piece: Denis Compton's bat, with which he scored all his runs in 1947, has pride of place at Lord's. As part of the redecoration of the Pavilion to celebrate the Bicentenary of Lord's, there will be new displays dedicated to the 150 years of Middlesex. Photo courtesy of MCC.

STYLE AND POLISH

Rob Steen remembers **Jack Robertson**, owner of the county's highest individual score and giver of sage batting advice

John Lyon School, deep in the bowels of Harrow Hill. First indoor net of the decade for the new boys. Memory, an increasingly unreliable source, insists it was raining; being a few days after Christmas it can be said with reasonable certainty that it was much warmer inside the heat-free precursor to the sports centre Mr Elizabeth Windsor would open 27 years later. At the bowler's end stands a slim, trim, unprepossessing figure with the air of a gown-less geography master.

He talks quietly but precisely, serving up crisp slices of philosophical and technical wisdom. If the exact words are lost in time's misty video replay, the message endures. "You don't have to wallop everything. Stretch that left leg and brace it. Head down. Sniff the ball. It's just as satisfying keeping a good ball out as clobbering a bad one. You might even enjoy it."

The man who taught me the intricacies and yes, the joy of the forward defensive seemed as far from a local hero as was possible to imagine. I'd been told he was the coach, an ex-Middlesex player from way back, but the name meant nothing until I consulted *Wisden* and *Playfair* when I got home. As his stature dawned, as I realised that this Jack Robertson was that Jack Robertson, my 12-year-old chest began heaving with pride.

It was January 1970. A decade had passed since Jack had retired as the (then) third-greediest run-hoarder in Seaxe history. A shade over two decades since that 331-in-a-day at New Road – still the highest score in club annals. Not one of us first-years had thought for a nanosecond to request his autograph. I was almost certainly the only one with his head buried in the yellow book that night.

There would be further sessions, further opportunities to badger. The questions queued up. What was it like sharing a dressing room with Compton and Edrich? Did Denis really turn up for play with sleepy bloodshot eyes and bow-tie laddishly skewiff? Did Bill – whose career had also stretched from 1937 to 1959 – really fly all those bombing missions and knock back all those pints?

How big were those sixes by Big Jim Sims? What was it like during Patsy's last days? How prescient were those first glimpses of Titmus? What was it really like in '47, that summer of gluttony and glory? How did it feel to rack up those nine century opening stands with Syd Brown, and set a club first-wicket record of 310 against Notts – and still be merely the *hors d'oeuvres*? What did it feel like to reach that maiden Test ton in Port of Spain? To open with Hutton? To score 331 in a day?

Sadly, my nerve failed me abysmally. Regrets? Too many to mention.

What strikes you most forcibly about Jack Robertson's career is the way Dame Fortune kept her distance. All told, 67 centuries and nearly 32,000 first-class runs flowed from that dapper bat yet he wound up with the same number of Test hundreds as Jack Russell (two). At the highest level he averaged more than Maurice Leyland, Dennis Amiss and David Gower (46.36) yet had the same number of Test outings as Tim Ambrose (11, of which just two came on home soil and the rest on minor tours). The chief causes were war and a bankable firm of openers, Len Hutton and Cyril Washbrook. Only three times did Jack kick off an England innings with the future Sir Len.

Picked, unproductively, at No.3 against South Africa in 1947, he opened in five Tests against West Indies and New Zealand in 1948 and 1949, collecting close to 600 runs, including two centuries. The second came at Lord's after he'd been drafted in to replace the injured Washbrook; not until the 1951-52 tour of India, with Hutton unavailable, did he see international action again. Four modest Tests were followed by twin top scores in Madras (77 and 56) but he could do nothing to prevent a heavy, series-clinching defeat – and that was his lot.

N DAVID BENBOW ROBERTSON

n: February 22, 1917, Chiswick
d: October 12, 1996, Bury St Edmunds
nt-hand batsman

,088 first-class runs (31,914 overall) at 38.36 for
ddlesex 1937–59
1 runs at 46.36 in 11 Tests
iddlesex cap 1939
sden Cricketer of the Year 1948
iddlesex benefit 1951, 1959

RES OF 250 AND ABOVE BY MIDDLESEX BATSMEN
FIRST-CLASS CRICKET

*	JDB Robertson	v Worcestershire	Worcester	1949
*	EH Hendren	v Worcestershire	Dudley	1933
*	JW Hearne	v Essex	Leyton	1929
*	EH Hendren	v Kent	Lord's	1922
*	WJ Edrich	v Northants	Northampton	1947
*	JD Carr	v Gloucestershire	Lord's	1994
	MW Gatting	v Somerset	Bath	1984
	WJ Edrich	v Leicestershire	Leicester	1947
*	DL Haynes	v Sussex	Lord's	1990
*	DCS Compton	v Somerset	Lord's	1948
*	FA Tarrant	v Essex	Leyton	1914

he year that Middlesex shared the Championship with
kshire, Robertson's unbeaten triple hundred enabled
tain George Mann to declare at the end of the first
at New Road with a whopping 623 for 5 on the board.
der the headline "Robertson trounces the Worcester
ling", *The Times* reported that Robertson "was at his
t all the way through. His timing of the ball enabled him
tinually to pierce the outfield and he was quick enough
his feet to get right to the pitch of the slow bowlers".
as the highest individual score in England since Len
ton's 364 in the Ashes Test at The Oval in 1938 and the
hest in the Championship since Eddie Paynter's 322 for
ncashire against Sussex a year earlier. Middlesex went
to beat Worcestershire by an innings and 54 runs.

Without filmic evidence, that renowned style and polish must be taken on trust. The most striking images in the photos are the firm, serious eyebrows and those dark, calm, calming eyes. The abiding impression is of a decent facsimile of another Jack; like Hobbs, it seems, here was a man possessed of the virtue all openers crave: serenity.

In 1947, John Arlott characterised Jack as "unobtrusive" but at the same time "a craftsman of stylish method and neat footwork", one widely considered the finest new-ball repeller in the land. "For all his modest bearing, he batted with an air of brisk mastery." Still more worthy of quotation is the Poet Laureate of Alderney's description of his second innings on that Test debut at The Oval – when, inevitably, he played second fiddle to Compton: "If Robertson felt inadequate in such a comparison – as, surely, any batsman in the world must have done – he dutifully ran Compton's runs (at least those called on the basis of reason) and gathered for himself such profits as offered."

Seldom can a sportsman's attributes have been captured with such painterly prose. Jack Robertson, the very essence of the team player, deserved every word. ●

Rob Steen has been following Middlesex since 1967. He revised for his A-levels in the Grand Stand then spent more than 20 years covering the county for The Guardian, The Independent, *the* Daily *and* Sunday Telegraph, *the* Sunday Times *and* Wisden Cricket Monthly.

INTERVIEW BY JOHN STERN

"THERE WERE NEVER ANY MEETINGS ABOUT WINNING"

Three Middlesex legends discuss post-war life at Lord's, batting with Compton and a more innocent age

I t is a glorious, cloudless day at Lord's in early May, the first day of Middlesex's Championship match against Surrey and three of the county's finest and longest-serving players have reconvened to reminisce: Alan Moss, whose fast bowling yielded 1,088 wickets for the county, peerless gloveman John 'JT' Murray, who is second in the all-time list of dismissals, and Peter Parfitt, the dashing batsman and super-snaffler of slip catches. It wouldn't be entirely correct to call the subject of discussion 'the good old days' because during the 1950s and 1960s, when these great men did their best work, Middlesex were trophy-less. But their careers, punctuated as they were by England appearances, were no less memorable or fascinating for that. And simply to be in their company, to have their ear, to listen and laugh at tales of Edrich and Compton, JW Hearne and Gubby Allen, of Gentlemen and Players, of have-a-go heroics and hapless timekeeping is a rare privilege. The anecdotes start flowing even before the tape recorder is switched on and long after it is turned off, over lunch in the Tavern.

Middlesex's young opener Sam Robson is being presented with his first-team cap during the lunch interval …
John Murray (Middlesex career 1952–75): Bill Edrich gave me my cap in the loo I think. He didn't actually give me a cap, he just told me.
Alan Moss (1950–63): Mine was nearly as bad. We were about to start a match. I don't know who was captain – they had a different one every match in those days – but he told everyone

that Don Bennett was being given his cap. "Congratulations Don." I said, "What about me?" "You've got yours. You've had yours ages." I said, "I haven't – I've got a load of bloody wickets but I haven't got a cap."

How did it all start for you?
Murray: I was due to come on to the MCC groundstaff when I was 14 and then they changed the school-leaving age to 15. I hadn't sat or passed an exam in my life. All I was interested in was playing cricket. Middlesex was the only county I could play for because of where I was born [Notting Hill].
Peter Parfitt (1956–72): I came from Norfolk and played for them as a schoolboy. Bill Edrich, who was also from there, asked me to come to Middlesex.
Murray: Al, you were an amateur old boy …
Moss: I was an apprentice carpenter and joiner for an outfit in Wembley. Unbeknown to me, the foreman lived next to a guy who ran a club called West Willesden Ramblers – no home, no nothing – and he asked me if I wanted to play cricket. Then they put me forward for the *Evening News* Colts, run by Lyn Wellings [journalist and former cricketer] at Alf Gover's cricket school. I owe everything to that start. I played a match at Lord's and was approached by two or three counties and I had to decide whether I was going to play cricket or carry on with carpentry and joining. Thanks goodness I made the right decision. It was difficult coming here because you were very much on your own. The nets were in the evenings and you would bowl

Back home: (left to right) John Murray, Alan Moss and Peter Parfitt at Lord's in May 2013

> **If certain amateurs turned up, the professionals would have to pack their bags and go home**

to the members and to amateur players like Freddie Brown and Norman Yardley who worked in the City. There was the Honourable Luke White, who played in one of the Victory Tests – I broke his jaw one time in the nets. That got me in the trap. But I was an amateur while I was in the Forces.

Murray: So you had your initials in front of your name on the scorecard? Not like the famous incident here when the public address announcer said: "Good morning ladies and gentlemen. There is one alteration to your scorecard. On the Middlesex team, FJ Titmus should read Titmus, FJ.

What sort of money did you earn back then?

Murray: When I first came I think we were paid match money then I did National Service from '53 to '55 and was retained by Middlesex. I think I got £2 a month as a

retainer, then you got match money when you played. In Mossy's early days Middlesex didn't exist as such. We were paid by MCC. It was only in '54 or '55 they started to pay us. [Middlesex didn't have their own office at Lord's until 1952.]

Moss: Where the Middlesex shop is now used to be a tea-house for the Harris Garden. You used to walk through to the office and fall through the floor because the floorboards were rotten. I never earned a thousand pounds a year. I'd have earned more as a fully-qualified joiner. I went on a few England tours then I started selling print through a Middlesex member. I ended up chairing a public company – that was all through cricket. Cricket gave me that chance.

Parfitt: I have to confess that I was concerned throughout my cricket career about what I was going to do when I finished playing. It worried me. I wasn't academically qualified to do anything. And when the opportunity came along to run a pub in 1972 I took it.

Murray: I was lucky enough to play until I was 40 but most people didn't. But I met a man, Derrick Robins, who gave me a job in the winters and I worked for him for six years when I was still playing. And then, true to his word, I went to work for him full time when I finished playing. I sold squash courts.

How did the relationship between amateurs and professionals work?

Moss: In the early days for the [professional] batters it was frightening. The amateurs would turn up in the school holidays. You'd go down to Hove and Syd Brown, Jack Robertson and the whole top five – excluding Compton and Edrich of course – would wait to see who came through the doors. And if certain amateurs turned up, they would have to pack their bags and go home.

Parfitt: Fred Titmus had a theory that the reason Yorkshire did so well year after year was because they didn't pander to the amateur as a lot of other counties did. John Dewes, who was teaching geography, used to walk straight in here and poor old Harry Sharp had to go and bowl in the nets.

Moss: We played at The Oval one time when JJ Warr was captain and I was in the pros' dressing room. I was the senior pro, about to retire and JJ said to me: "There's no room in there, come on in with us." So I took my bags in, put them down and then Peter May [Surrey captain] walked in, took JJ aside and said: "I'm sorry, JJ, Mossy can't stay in here."

Murray: You can't believe it, can you? And Peter May was such a nice lad. We were playing at Northampton one time and most of the boys had already gone but Don Bick and I ended up getting the same train as Walter Robins [the captain]. He was travelling first-class and would get dinner. We were on the lower deck with all the baggage. There was no question of us getting any dinner.

Moss: That was a run, that was. Coming off the field at Lord's and having to get straight on a train up north. You'd be stinking wet, no time for a shower. You had to pack your bags, get in a cab and get straight to the station.

During the eras that you played in, Middlesex's results did not match up to the talent on the field. Why do you think that was?

Moss: It was terrible. I never won a thing.

Murray: Titmus always blamed me. I came here in '50 and Middlesex had won the Championship in '49. I left in '75 and

then we won it again in '76. He said, "Now I know what's been wrong with us all these years!" Up until when Bill and Denis finished in about '58 we never set out to win a Championship. There were never any meetings about winning. I could understand it with Bill in many ways. He had survived six years of war, low-flying bombing raids and gets a DFC. And now he's playing cricket again so he ain't too bothered about whether he wins the Championship. All he's interested in is …

Moss: … being alive …

Murray: … and what sort of party are we going to have at the Mere Country Club this Saturday night! It only got serious about twice a year – when we played Yorkshire and Surrey.

Parfitt: That sort of attitude lingered on even when JJ Warr was captain. In 1959 Guinness had put up some money for the side who scored the quickest 200 and our sole purpose if we won the toss was to win that money – and we did win it. In the same season we played Somerset at Bath. We were holding our own in the Championship and JJ said: "As far as I can tell everybody's much of a muchness so we'll draw for the batting order with a pack of cards." And I came out No. 9.

> **QUICK MONEY**
> Middlesex beat Kent by 109 runs at Gravesend in May 1959. In the second innings Ron Hooker and Bob Gale hit maiden hundreds and thrashed the fastest 200 of the season to bring in £500 for the team. Kent, set 294, held out until "five minutes from the end of extra time", according to *Wisden* who also declared: "Not even the sternest critic of modern cricket would have faulted this match."

Murray: Our coach back then was Jack Hearne, JW Hearne.

Moss: He used to stand by the net in his mac and say "For-ward … for-ward" to the batsman.

Murray: There was a lot of debate at the time – as there always is – about walking and JJ, the captain, has given us a bit of a lecture up in the dressing room at the start of the season: "Boys, we're going to walk." Jack was sitting in the corner, still in his mac and trilby. JJ said to Jack: "Isn't that right, Jack W?" He said: "I never walked in my f****** life, captain." That was the end of that. Most players walked, though.

Moss: It's strange how it all went about. JJ was talking as a bowler but batsmen didn't want to walk. Len Hutton didn't walk, Cyril Washbrook didn't walk.

What did you make of the captains you played under?

Murray: JJ wasn't a good captain off the field but on the field he was in my top two.

Moss: Shrewd operator.

Murray: Walter Robins was a good captain. He captained the second XI one year and he would deliberately not turn up on time. One of the senior pros would take us out on the field and then suddenly someone would say: "He's here." "Where?" "Behind that tree." Eventually he'd come out and whatever had been happening – successful or not – he changed everything, put new bowlers on and changed the field.

Moss: Always wore a trilby and a waistcoat. He was a good reader of the game. He never talked rubbish unlike some of the ones we had. Ian Bedford wasn't bad. They brought him back because he was a leg-spinner and because they didn't want a pro as captain.

Parfitt: He would consult, he would ask. I did it for two years and in retrospect I would have been better off not doing it [Parfitt was captain from 1968–70]. One thing you've got to have is co-operation from the players on the field. Without that you've got no chance.

What was Denis Compton like?

Murray: He wasn't easy. I played in '52 because his brother Leslie was injured. He didn't welcome me with open arms. He could be difficult though we became very good friends over time.

Moss: He was gifted. He had incredible ability. He would have murdered Twenty20. He didn't hit sixes. I remember seeing him squirt boundaries down to third man despite two fielders being there. Charlie Knott, the Hampshire off-spinner, pretty much retired after Denis made a hundred against him in 1954. But you wouldn't want to be batting at the other end.

Parfitt: I played a few games with him and I had one experience at Glastonbury. When I went in he could only have had a dozen. An hour and a quarter later he had 110 and I still wasn't into double figures. I perceived him to be like all great players that I played with – if they fancied the bowling then you're standing at the bowler's end all day; if they didn't fancy it, then you're the one who's trying to get down the other bloody end!

Moss: Jack Robertson and Syd Brown would say that once Edrich came in he would start nicking the bowling and when Compton came in they wouldn't see a ball.

> **" Denis was gifted. He had incredible ability. He would have murdered Twenty20**

Murray: Denis (bottom-right) had played 80 or 90 Tests so on a Wednesday at Ashby de la Zouch or Northampton, places like that, he didn't want to be there. How often would you hear him telling Titmus to toss it up – "Come on Fred, toss it up" – because he was bored. And Fred was trying to keep it tight. Fred used to tell him to p*** off. Yorkshire and Surrey – then he would try a bit.

Parfitt: He did surprise me once. It was not long after I had started. He came and sat down beside me on the balcony. He didn't really converse with us much and if he wanted to get on the shove ha'penny board you got off. He put his hand on my leg and said to me: "Peter, you just enjoy your cricket because it'll be over before you know it's even begun." And I've often reflected on that.

My brother played a bit for Norfolk with Bill Edrich and Bill was holding court one day about when he had been a pilot in a Blenheim. They scrambled and Bill got up on the wing and realised that he'd forgotten his parachute. But he just said "F*** it and carried on."

Moss: Apparently a lot of crews wouldn't fly with Bill because he used to fly so low – "they can't get me down here, he'd say". He was almost done for dangerous flying.

Murray: An example of his courage was a game in 1954 at Lord's against Northamptonshire when Frank Tyson was trying break into the England side. His run-up was enormous. Northants had been bowled out and Middlesex had a period of time to bat at the end of the second day. Jack Robertson was out and Bill went in. Frank gave him a bouncer which Bill tried to hook. He got a top edge and into his face. They carried him off and he had to have his jaw wired up. He was being fed by a straw. The next morning, the dressing-room door opened and in walks Edrich with all this stuff around his face and starts getting changed. Denis asks him what he thinks he's doing? And at the fall of the next wicket, Bill went in. The first ball from Tyson wasn't a bouncer but it was short and he took it on the chest. He only lasted about 10 minutes but it showed the character of the man.

All three of you played in a match against Kent at Tunbridge Wells in June 1963 that Wisden *described as "without parallel in the history of first-class cricket" – can you explain what happened?*

Murray: We'd bowled Kent out and at stumps on the Saturday night we're 121 for 3. We all went home because we weren't playing on the Sunday and we came back on the Monday morning. Mossy was senior pro so it was his car that we had to go in – how much were you getting per mile? – and it was decided that we should meet at Baker Street station. There's me, Mossy and Don Bennett. Off we go. We get to Tonbridge and there's a bit of traffic. To get into Tunbridge Wells you have to go down a big hill. At the top of this hill the traffic is single file and everything's come to a stop but we're not bothered because Mossy's No.11, I'm seven and Bennett's eight. We were inching along when Mossy sees something in the mirror and says: "There's some stupid bastard coming down the outside." This car absolutely flew past and it turned out it was numbers four, five and six in the batting order [Bob White, Ron Hooker and Fred Titmus] – oh s***. We didn't get there in time and as we drove into the ground Jim Sims, our scorer, stood there and said to you: "Alan, there's a crisis."

We had to declare because we only had three players there for the start. We all scrambled to get out there and Kent gave us five fielders. John Prodger, their batsman, was fielding at first slip and dived full length to catch Brian Luckhurst.

We were summoned to Gubby Allen's flat in Kensington on the Tuesday night.

Parfitt: It transpired that according to the laws of the game, Colin Cowdrey, the Kent captain, could have asked the umpires to delay the game by half an hour.

Moss: I had a stand-up row with Cowdrey. I asked Jim [the scorer] what the situation was and he said that we had to declare. I said no, no and the whole thing got out of hand. Cowdrey was insisting that we had to declare.

Murray: Another thing happened in that match that I've never seen before. Peter Richardson in the second innings got to 95, played forward to Titmus, I caught it and threw it back to Fred and he walked off. No one appealed. He just said it had brushed his glove. ●

THE LATE, LATE SHOW

At Tunbridge Wells, June 15, 17, 18, 1963. Drawn. Kent 150 (FJ Titmus 4-39, RW Hooker 4-57) and 341-7 dec. (PE Richardson 95, SE Leary 92*, JM Prodger 74); Middlesex 121-3 dec. (Parfitt 54) and 82-3.

Wisden reported: "The late arrival on Monday morning of nine of the Middlesex team, including Drybrough, the captain, provided a situation without parallel in the history of first-class cricket. At the close on Saturday, Middlesex, having dismissed Kent for 150, were 121 for three wickets with White 43 not out, Hooker 13 not out. The team had stayed at a local hotel on Friday night and arranged to do the same on Monday night, but they returned to their London homes at the weekend.

"Three players arrived at the ground with plenty of time to spare. They were White and S. E. Russell, who had already been dismissed, and Clark, the twelfth man. White put on his pads and gloves and waited on the boundary, hoping his partner would be in time while the umpires and the Kent players went to the middle. After a wait of a liberal two minutes, the umpires led the players off the field and it was officially stated that the umpires had closed the Middlesex innings.

"It was decided that Kent should begin their second innings within ten minutes and Cowdrey agreed that Clark could keep wicket while if necessary White and S. E. Russell shared the bowling, Kent providing sufficient substitute fielders to make up eleven in the field for Middlesex. Actually, Underwood, Catt, Prodger, Brown and Dye assisted their opponents, but within three overs the whole Middlesex side were present and fielding."

CAUGHT ON CAMERA

In 1975, his final season, JT Murray broke Herbert Strudwick's world record for first-class dismissals (since broken and still held by Bob Taylor). *Wisden* asserts that the key wicket was Richard Lewis of Hampshire but the recollection of those involved was that the moment came in the previous match at Lord's against Surrey.

Murray remembers it as a regulation outside edge – DR Owen-Thomas c Murray b Lamb 7: "That's right – Dudley Owen-Thomas of KCS Wimbledon and Cambridge University, bowled by the Honourable Timothy Lamb of Shrewsbury School and Oxford University, caught by John Murray of St John's Church of England School, Notting Hill. And Titmus always asked – who's the odd man out?"

The wicket was one of six taken in the innings by Tim Lamb,

MOST FIRST-CLASS DISMISSALS

	Career	Mat	Dis	Ct	St
RW Taylor	1960–88	639	1649	1473	176
JT Murray	1952–75	635	1527	1268	259
H Strudwick	1902–27	674	1495	1237	258
APE Knott	1964–85	511	1344	1211	133
RC Russell	1981–2004	465	1320	1192	128

who recalls: "In anticipation that the record might be broken that morning Fred Titmus had secreted a camera in the square-leg umpire's pocket so when the moment arrived and all the players celebrated, Fred snapped it."

Three of the best: (left to right) Murray, Parfitt and Moss

ALAN EDWARD MOSS

Born: November 14, 1930, Tottenham
Right-arm fast-medium bowler, right-hand batsman

- 1,088 first-class wickets for Middlesex at 19.81 1950–63
- Eighth in all-time list of Middlesex wicket-takers
- 21 wickets in 9 Tests at 29.80
- Took more than 100 first-class wickets in a season five times (best 136 at 13.72 in 1960)
- Middlesex cap 1952
- Middlesex benefit 1962
- Middlesex committee 1976–2010; executive board member 2010–12
- Middlesex Cricket Board chairman 1996–2010
- Middlesex treasurer 1984–93; chairman 1995–99; president 2003–05

JOHN THOMAS MURRAY

Born: April 1, 1935, North Kensington
Right-hand batsman, wicketkeeper

- Broke world record for most first-class dismissals in 1975 (now second in all-time list)
- One of only two keepers (the other is Les Ames) to score 1,000 runs and make 100 first-class dismissals in a season
- Effected more than 70 first-class dismissals in a season seven times
- 1,024 catches (1,268 overall) and 200 stumpings (259 overall) for Middlesex 1952–75
- 15,251 runs (18,872 overall) for Middlesex at 23.24
- 2,268 one-day runs for Middlesex at 19.55
- Middlesex debut 1952, aged 17
- Middlesex cap 1956
- Middlesex benefit 1966, 1975
- Wisden Cricketer of the Year 1967
- 21 Tests for England 1961–67
- Awarded MBE 1976
- Member of Middlesex committee 1979-2000

PETER HOWARD PARFITT

Born: December 8, 1936, Billingford, Norfolk
Left-hand batsman

- 21,302 first-class runs (26,924 overall) for Middlesex at 36.66, 46 hundreds
- 1,882 runs in 37 Tests at 40.91, 7 hundreds
- Passed 1,000 first-class runs in a season 14 times including 2,000-plus three times
- Scored 2,007 runs just for Middlesex in 1961
- Took 40 or more catches in a season for Middlesex four times
- Third in list of all-time first-class catchers (non keepers) for Middlesex with 453 behind Clive Radley (485) and Patsy Hendren (566)
- Middlesex cap 1960
- Wisden Cricketer of the Year 1963
- Middlesex captain 1968–70
- Middlesex benefit 1970
- Middlesex president 2009-11

LEGEND OF LONGEVITY

Fred Titmus started his career as a teenager and finished it when he was almost 50.
Terry Cooper profiles Middlesex's greatest servant and one of England's best spinners

Fred Titmus lives on. Late last season there he was – one of our county's genuine greats – getting yet more mentions in the media three decades after his final retirement. One of his successors as the county's off-spinner, Ollie Rayner, had produced match-figures of 15 for 118 against Surrey at The Oval. Spectacular stuff, but not quite as good as Fred, because it was noted that Rayner's analysis was Middlesex's best since Fred's 15 for 95 against Somerset at Bath in 1955.

Middlesex contrived to lose at Bath back then but at least Rayner's marvellous bowling brought victory. Fred's first-class career began at Bath when he made his debut aged 16 – sixteen! – years, seven months. He had been on the Lord's groundstaff for a few weeks when Middlesex were looking for someone to fill gaps left by having five players selected for a Test. Those emperors of the game, Gubby Allen and Walter Robins, saw Fred crashing the ball about in the nets and next morning he was on the first train west.

His home was in Kentish Town – a bus-ride from Lord's and also a short hop from William Ellis Grammar School. In an otherwise heavily built-up area the school was happily on the edge of Parliament Hill Fields, opening onto Hampstead Heath – London's lungs. I can vouch for the fact that the open spaces were a sports-mad boy's paradise.

The library overlooked an enclosed cricket ground, with nets. Within a couple of hundred yards there was an athletics track, banks of tennis courts, multiple football pitches and more cricket facilities. Fred could not help perfecting his

talents so that he was fully ready when he was accepted by the Lord's groundstaff and then had a 22-match season, still only 17, alongside those giants Denis Compton and Bill Edrich when Middlesex signed him for 1950.

Around the time of his Test debut in 1955, a couple of school-mates and I went to Lord's – free entry after tea, what bliss. Autograph books handy, we accosted Fred at the pavilion door. "Old school tie, I see," he said and asked us how we were getting on, when we wanted to say: "Less about us, what about you?"

The headmaster had proudly announced Fred's first cap. "I wish to draw to the attention of the school that F. Titmus, formerly of Cumberland House, has been nominated to play for England in the forthcoming Test match." Glad he told us. Mind you, a previous head had sincerely hoped: "You're not considering a career in sport, Titmus, are you?" Error of judgement there.

He had to play for England that year, even though Jim Laker and Roy Tattersall were established, as he was in the process of taking 191 wickets and amassing 1,235 runs, thus achieving the first of his eight doubles – the same as WG Grace. It was a brief introduction to Tests. Like Ken Barrington in the same series, he was omitted for several years before both came back to have memorable Test careers, Fred resuming Tests in 1962. By that time he had become the "wily old fox" rather than "young Freddie, the Cockney battler."

FREDERICK JOHN TITMUS

Born: November 24, 1932, Somers Town
Died: March 23, 2011, Hemel Hempstead
Right-arm off-spin bowler, Right-hand batsman,

- 2,361 first-class wickets (2,830 overall) for Middlesex 1949–82
- 146 5-fors (168 overall), 23 10-wicket matches (26 overall)
- 17,320 first-class runs (21,588 overall) for Middlesex at 22.78, 5 hundreds
- 153 wickets at 32.22 in 53 Tests
- Middlesex cap 1953
- Wisden Cricketer of the Year 1963
- Middlesex benefit 1963, 1973
- Middlesex captain 1965–68
- Tenth in list of all-time first-class wicket-takers
- Scored 1,000 runs and took 100 wickets in a season eight times
- Only four other men have scored 20,000 runs and taken 2,500 wickets: WG Grace, George Hirst, Wilfred Rhodes and Maurice Tate

MOST FIRST-CLASS WICKETS IN A SEASON FOR MIDDLESEX

158	FJ Titmus	1955
154	AE Trott	1900
150	AE Trott	1899
145	JT Hearne	1893
143	CIJ Smith	1934

MOST FIRST-CLASS FIVE-WICKET HAULS FOR MIDDLESEX

171	JT Hearne
146	FJ Titmus
89	FA Tarrant
88	JW Hearne
77	JM Sims

MOST FIRST-CLASS WICKETS FOR MIDDLESEX

2,361	FJ Titmus
2,093	JT Hearne
1,438	JW Hearne
1,257	JM Sims
1,250	JE Emburey

MOST FIRST-CLASS APPEARANCES FOR MIDDLESEX

642	FJ Titmus	1949–82
581	EH Hendren	1907–37
520	CT Radley	1964–87
508	JT Murray	1952–75
465	JW Hearne	1909–36

> " When not bowling, Fred joined Murray and Parfitt in constant chatter in the slips, sometimes louder than intended because of Fred's slight deafness

He was now a master bowler, with a short, sashaying run, the merest hop and a high, slightly deceptive, minute check before delivery. His line was straightness personified and he turned the ball adequately or sharply. His ace was what he called the "swinger", a drifter or arm-ball. Batsmen knew the ball might float away, but they had to play because it might pitch and turn back.

Keeper John Murray and slips Peter Parfitt and Clive Radley created a cottage industry happily collecting the edges. When not bowling, Fred joined Murray and Parfitt in constant chatter in the slips, sometimes louder than intended because of Fred's slight deafness. So you could sit in the Grand Stand and be an eaves-dropper on some juicy gossip. An early captain, John Warr, said: "Fred often takes catches in mid-conversation."

Let's not forget his batting. He started as a batting all-rounder, with the style expected of an MCC graduate. Ted Dexter was happy to promote him to opener at the start of the 1964 Ashes when John Edrich trod on a ball before the toss. He liked to attack and hit over mid-on powerfully. His cutting could be fearsome. I remember one explosive, flat square-cut for six at Lord's. Think Gordon Greenidge or Robin Smith. The ball stayed about four feet high and rifled through the promenaders – who in those days could stand on the concourse in front of the old Tavern – before damaging the pub's brickwork. Bodies hit the deck and there were broken beer glasses everywhere. The dilemma was whether to renew your beer or order a stiff brandy to calm the nerves.

> " He would bowl any time – with the wind or against it, uphill or downhill, with no wickets down or with lots gone

Fred was not communicative with the press when captain. Reasons for team changes had to be dragged out of him. One typical injury report was simply: "If he were a horse we'd have to shoot him." Like all other players he decided that 59 steps up to the old press box in the Warner Stand was too much of a climb. Phil Edmonds was an exception. He always wanted to get his version of any talking-point in first.

But Fred was a willing communicator with supporters – anything better than silence. Some of us went to Swansea for a top-of-the-table game and, in the bar the night before, a couple of us said how well a quick win would suit us as we had to work on the Friday. Fred's spin wrapped it up inside two days and when we paused at the dressing room he asked: "All right, chaps? Any time you want a favour, just mention it."

During the 1960s a batch of Middlesex players followed Fred by earning Test caps: Murray, Parfitt, John Price, Eric Russell. Despite this talent, the county maddeningly under-achieved. Between 1962 and 1975 their highest in the championship was sixth.

Fred was given the chance to improve results in 1965. He was unsuccessful and resigned during his fourth season. In his memoirs he recalled: "I felt that I was playing with the weight of the world on my shoulders and when I took the decision the enormous weight had been lifted."

Clive Radley joined just before Fred's captaincy began and remembers: "Fred was brilliant to me. He taught me everything about approach and attitude. It was not technical stuff, just how to look after myself. I travelled with him in his Beetle, but just sat in the back seat and listened. After about five years I summoned the nerve to say: 'Why do we always go up the A1 to Yorkshire? What about the M1?' 'I know all about that M1. The A1's flatter. Save yourself half a gallon of fuel,' he said.

"As captain he was tactically excellent, but his man-management was not the greatest. But it was a hard school and he was a hard task-master. When Brearley came back as captain they didn't get on. Couldn't see eye to eye about much at all, though in the cause of cutting costs they did share a tent at Scarborough instead of wasting cash on a hotel."

Always ready: Fred Titmus bowls against Nottinghamshire at Lord's during his five-match comeback in 1980. Substitute fielder Ian Gould is at mid-off and the non-striker is Basher Hassan

THE COMEBACK KING

COMEBACK NO.1 – 1980

With John Emburey on England duty and Phil Edmonds having knee surgery, Titmus, aged 47, played five Championship matches in 1980 and in doing so became the first man to play first-class cricket in five different decades. Vince van der Bijl remembers the first one against Yorkshire: "In the second innings Phil Carrick, who was a fantastic player of spin, came down the wicket to Fred and hit him hard,

a 'line drive', through mid-on. Roland Butcher ran two yards to his left, dived full length and took the ball inches off the turf. We were all relieved, and I ran from leg gully to Fred, gave him a hug and just said: 'Great Fred.' And he said to me very quietly with a twinkle in his eye: 'I just gave that one a bit more air.'" **John Stern**

At Scarborough, July 23, 24, 25, 1980. Middlesex 391 (RO Butcher 179, CT Radley 65; GB Stevenson 5-84) and 101-2; Yorkshire 118 (MWW Selvey 4-39, FJ Titmus 6.3-2-8-1) and, following on, 370 (DL Bairstow 145, JH Hampshire 67; WW Daniel 4-114, Titmus 32-7-82-2). Middlesex won by 8 wickets.

COMEBACK NO.2 – 1982

Mike Brearley on Titmus's final match, aged 49: "It was Clive Radley's idea. We were playing Surrey at Lord's in August, the pitch was dry and had probably been used twice before. Fred had popped into the dressing room for a cup of tea and Clive just said: 'Get him to play.' 'Good idea'. And Philippe Edmonds hurt his back in the second innings. We set them 160 to win in about two and a quarter hours, Fred took three wickets and we won the match. It was one of those great games." **JS**

At Lord's, August 25, 26, 27, 1982. Middlesex 276 (WN Slack 79; KS Mackintosh 6-61) and 157-2 dec. (Slack 71*, KP Tomlins 51); Surrey 273-4 dec. (GP Howarth 112, AR Butcher 82; FJ Titmus 15-3-49-0) and 102 (JE Emburey 13.3-2-24-4, Titmus 10-1-43-3). Middlesex won by 58 runs.

Their strained relationship was activated on the field, where Fred wanted over-riding control as the bowler. Parfitt recalls: "Mike was at mid-wicket but said that he'd go to forward short-leg. Fred said twice 'I don't want you there.' Brears said 'Just for the over, Fred.' The next ball was a full toss that was pulled past his head like a tracer bullet."

Wicketkeeper Murray approved. "Quite right. Fred was never going to let people set his fields. He was the best bowler I kept to." (In context, JT also kept to Brian Statham and Fred Trueman.) "He would bowl any time – with the wind or against it, uphill or downhill, with no wickets down or with lots gone. He always wanted to bowl. He believed that if he took 100 wickets he would get another contract, He knew his strike-rate was one wicket every ten overs, and he reckoned that if he bowled 1,000 overs he would get his 100. So he always wanted to bowl."

He played plenty of Tests in the 1960s until, as he laconically put it: "My tour of the West Indies ended when I had four toes chopped off by the propeller of a motorboat." That was in February 1968, but he was bowling away at the first match at Derby in May, took 111 wickets in the season and topped Middlesex's batting averages. But the toe accident caused another hiatus in his England career, though he was restored at the age of 42 to face Lillee and Thomson.

He was dropped by Middlesex in 1976 but returned to contribute to that season's Championship title. He retired on the back of that triumph, though there were a few brief comebacks, notably in 1982 when he was press-ganged into action on a chance visit to Lord's, took 3 for 43 against Surrey and helped seal another title. What a career. ●

Terry Cooper, a Middlesex member since 1965, reported on the county for the Press Association and Wisden *over 25 years*

DIAMONDS ARE A CAPTAIN'S BEST FRIEND

The Guardian's **Mike Selvey** pays tribute to **Wayne Daniel**, his former new-ball partner and Middlesex's most fearsome overseas player

MICHAEL WALTER WILLIAM SELVEY

Born: April 25, 1948, Chiswick

Right-arm fast-medium bowler, right-hand batsman

- 615 first-class wickets (772 overall) at 25.45 for Middlesex 1972–82
- 294 one-day wickets (333 overall) for Middlesex
- 101 first-class wickets at 19.09 in 1978
- 6 wickets in 3 Tests for England
- Middlesex 1972–82
- Middlesex cap 1973
- Middlesex benefit 1982
- Four County Championship titles
- Two one-day trophies
- Also played for Surrey and Glamorgan

Ever since he joined us we knew him as our Black Diamond, but it was Mike Smith who saw him in more pragmatic terms. "Rent and rates," he said, "he'll be guaranteeing my rent and rates." He knew which side his bread was buttered did Smudger, but then didn't we all. There was no disappointment either: 685 first class wickets for Middlesex at 22 apiece and 316 at 17 in one-day cricket speaks eloquently enough of his value. So do the four County Championships he helped earn and five one-day titles as well. When the Diamond was around, bowling at warp-factor speed or wearing his towel and sitting by the dressing-room door waiting, usually in vain, for some lovely to call him up on the payphone next to which he had parked himself, the rent and rates got paid.

We welcomed him with open arms. He was our nuclear option. Even back towards the start of the decade, it was irksome to find other counties with what became known as whizz-bangs. Hang around too long against Essex for example and you'd hear Tonker Taylor's growl: "Come and 'ave a bowl, KD." And on would come Keith Boyce and bounce the crap out of anyone until they capitulated. We didn't have that option. I could wobble it around at fast-medium but I only bowled bouncers at people who didn't hook (no runs conceded and Brearley happy because I was being "aggressive") and briefly Allan Jones bowled pretty briskly until his back went. But the Diamond was different class. He had been around a little on a Young West Indies trip in 1974, was spotted by the great Don

> **" Wayne could bowl fast. Well to be truthful, he didn't know how to bowl slow, even in the nets, which is more to the point**

we relished him, on the way to becoming one of the most valuable of all overseas players ever to play county cricket.

Wayne could bowl fast. Well to be truthful, he didn't know how to bowl slow, even in the nets, which is more to the point. Every delivery carried with it the weight of a cannonball, something that could jar the bat and send electric shocks down the nerves of the arm. And he bowled a horrible length, the tickler that could rattle the ribcage. All this he did from a most powerful virile action. I can picture it now: he pawed the turf first of all, running on the spot for a few steps before setting off on a hustling run. It was a big unit to get started and an even more difficult one to stop, for this was a boxer's build and no lightweight either. He leapt through the crease, wrist cocked, bowling arm high, front arm higher still. Then came the grunt of the effort and his right knuckle so low in follow-through that it all but scraped the ground. Just once this saved him from … well, goodness knows what the repercussions would have been had his head been up as Clive Lloyd's thunderous straight drive flew back at him. It seared past where his head ought by rights to have been, rose scarcely ten feet in the air at its apex before splintering a hole in the Old Trafford sightscreen. Even Wayne went quiet at that.

Only once did I see him angry and only once did we become concerned about his bowling. The first occasion was the Gillette Cup semi-final at Hove in 1980. For some reason best known to himself, Imran Khan, steaming at full throttle down the slope, decided to bounce Wayne. The Diamond was apoplectic. He took 6 for 15. Our

Bennett and played for our second team the following year. He might have joined us in 1976 but instead was there at the genesis of the West Indies war machine, with Andy Roberts and Michael Holding part of perhaps the first lethal triumvirate the game has seen.

Then we had a stroke of luck: Wayne joined World Series. Two years disappeared from his international life, and in that time, the fast men began to drop from the Caribbean production line. Wayne was on the West Indies periphery but he was ours now and how concern on the other occasion was more to do with the manner of his bowling, which was seeing him driven down the ground rather more than was seemly for someone of his calibre and reputation. After a few weeks of this, he confessed to us that *The Sun* newspaper was offering £500 to the Demon Bowler, he who hit the stumps most often during the season, and that he had his eyes on it. We offered to club together, and double it even, if he was just to start pebble-dashing batsmen again. There was no second bidding needed. We never paid him, mind. ●

> " I was sitting in a deckchair at Hove and as I saw the ball come down from Imran I just thought, 'Oh. That's probably not the best thing I've ever seen done'

"ONE OF THE GREATEST SPECTACLES I'VE SEEN"

The day that one overseas legend wound up another and paid the price

In August 1980 wicketkeeper Ian Gould, now one of the ICC's elite umpires, was on the point of leaving Middlesex – following the arrival of Paul Downton from Kent – to join Sussex. As the two sides came head to head at Hove in the semi-final of the 60-over Gillette Cup, he was just an interested observer.

"Wayne – just the mention of his name is making my hands sore again," says Gould over a black coffee and a cigarette before donning his white coat to umpire a Middlesex home game against Somerset. "I was sitting in a deckchair at Hove and as I saw the ball come down from Imran I just thought, 'Oh. That's probably not the best thing I've ever seen done.' And then seeing Wayne's helmet come flying off, I was thinking I wouldn't fancy batting against him after this.

"No one said a word to him – they didn't have to. He just put his boots on and went out there. It was one of the greatest spectacles I've seen. Oh my God. Wayne had terrorised Sussex before.

Payback: Imran Khan bounces Wayne Daniel at Hove in 1980. Daniel responded with a match-winning 6 for 15

He'd had Stuart Storey caught at cover, gloved off his chin. And their No.11 Giles Cheatle had been out hit wicket, except he wasn't. It's just we couldn't get him back because he was frightened senseless.

"Dear old Wayne did the job, as he always did. It's between him and Malcolm Marshall for the best overseas player I've ever seen. He hasn't changed a bit apart from white hair that makes him look like a pint of Guinness.

"He was a legend here and changed the whole environment. He'd sit in the corner and reminisce about his night before, which we all knew were lies because we'd been with him at the time. He is a charming, lovely man and if Middlesex have anyone to thank, it's him."
John Stern

Gillette Cup semi-final, Hove, August 13, 14, 1980. Middlesex beat Sussex by 64 runs. Middlesex 179 all out (60 overs) (MW Gatting 32; GG Arnold 3-17, GS Le Roux 3-40) Sussex 115 all out (49.2 overs) (WW Daniel 6-15).

"THE MOST GORGEOUS OF MEN"

Winning feeling: Wayne Daniel and Vince van der Bijl after the 1980 Gillette Cup final victory over Surrey

Middlesex reunion: (left to right) Mike Selvey, Vince van der Bijl, Wayne Daniel, Roland Butcher and Ian Gould together again for the first time in 30 years, in Barbados in 2010

WAYNE WENDELL DANIEL

Born: January 16, 1956, St Philip, Barbados

Right-arm fast bowler, right-hand batsman

- 685 first-class wickets (867 overall) at 22.02 for Middlesex 1977–88
- 36 wickets at 25.27 in 10 Tests for West Indies
- 316 one-day wickets for Middlesex at 17.41
- Middlesex cap 1977
- Middlesex benefit 1985
- Four County Championship titles
- Five one-day trophies
- Took 50 or more first-class wickets in nine of first ten seasons with Middlesex. Most was 79 at 26.72 in 1985
- Best bowling 9 for 61 v Glamorgan at Swansea, June 1982
- Took hat-trick v Lancashire, Southport, July 1981

Former Middlesex fast bowler Alan Moss was a member of the committee when Daniel joined Middlesex: "Don Bennett was coach and said: 'Come round the nets and have a look at this young man we're interested in – he's a bit quick'. I stood behind the net, Wayne bowled and I thought it was going to come through the net at me – very rarely do you get that. He was so bloody quick. So Don, typically cautious, said: 'I think he's all right.' 'All right?' I said. 'You want to sign him up before the others do.' They were still umming and aahing."

His new-ball partner in the double-winning season of 1980, Vince van der Bijl: "Wayne Daniel is just the most gorgeous of men. Generous, engaging but on the field fearsome. In 1981 I was in the UK on business and I popped into Maidstone where Middlesex were playing. I walked into the dressing room as they walked off for lunch and Wayne said 'Hey Vince, I've had something in my bag for a long time that I wanted to show you.' It was a cartoon of two yobbos going into a pub and this huge barman wearing a T-shirt that said 'Free Mandela'. And the two yobbos say to the barman" 'We'll have two pints of Mandela please'. A special man, Diamond." **JS**

"THE WELCOME WAS ALWAYS SO WARM"

From his home in Barbados, **Wayne Daniel** looks back on his great Middlesex career

My first season in 1977 was clouded with doubt for me because I had just come off a back injury which I had picked up at The Oval in 1976. I had missed the West Indies-Pakistan series at home and I was really worried. But the Middlesex doctor passed me fit.

I don't think I bowled at top pace that year, I was just feeling my way [He took 75 wickets at 16].

I had some battles against Nottinghamshire. I remember playing against 'Pasty' Harris – he was a big tough-looking guy. And he was flinching, threw the bat down a couple of times and gave me some very nasty looks, some nasty stares. I was really shaking him up. [Harris retired hurt 0, and Daniel took five wickets in both innings, his first five-fors for Middlesex].

Ian Gould always reminds me about that Gillette semi-final at Hove. It was a packed house at Sussex and in all my years of playing I never saw faces as glum as the Sussex supporters' that day. They were so disheartened but it was a great win for Middlesex.

I arrived at Middlesex as a youngster who could bowl really, really fast. But I learned a lot about control from guys like Phil Edmonds and John Emburey who kept instilling this toughness in me. If I was a bit tired and they felt that the batsmen were having it too easy, they would say: "No … no! You have to be at these guys all the time." These guys were mean – they didn't believe in giving batsmen any respite.

Brearley had his own way of showing his dislike for what you were doing. He would stand at first slip with his hands on his hips and just stare down the pitch.

I had raw pace, raw talent, but the tough professionalism became part of me from being around those guys.

I was very disappointed not to be part of the West Indies tour to England in 1980. When West Indies played Middlesex at Lord's I went into their dressing room and Malcolm Marshall said to me: "Really and truly you should have been on this tour." But I was with Middlesex and I intended to do my best for them.

Vince [van der Bijl] was a great help. You had this guy at other end who could land the ball on a pinhead. He was fantastic. So I felt that I had to match him. You couldn't let the pressure off. That was a really tremendous season.

I had a great relationship with Vince and Norman Featherstone. I couldn't believe these were two guys who came from apartheid South Africa. 'Feathers' and I would travel together to matches and I used to go to his place in Swiss Cottage or West Hampstead. It was so normal. I showed them the respect that they showed me. Vince would always have a drink in the pub.

I never looked at the colour of anyone's skin. My thing was to be competitive with the ball in my hand, to get you out, maybe even to rip your throat out. My job was to be aggressive and intimidating. I was the same when I was bowling to Viv Richards or Gordon Greenidge.

It was special to bowl at guys like Viv and Clive Lloyd. I was never a regular in the West Indies team so I always wanted to show that I was good enough to be part of their team. If you weren't on your game they made you look really, really stupid.

My best bowling figures were 9 for 61, down at Swansea. I remember being really tired and Harry Sharp, the scorer, said to me: "Come on, you've got to go out there and win the game for Middlesex." I said, "Oh Sharpy, I'm gonna try." "You're not gonna try, you've got to go out there and win the game."

I think I helped Norman Cowans (right) a great deal. I first met him when he was on the MCC groundstaff

and whenever I went to the nets he would come up and have a chat. He always wanted to talk about fast bowling and find out what it was really like to play first-class cricket. Then some evenings we'd go to the Tavern. I'd buy him pints of Guinness and say to him: "You gotta get strong, boy!" He was a skinny rake at that time. Then he joined Middlesex and we spent a lot of time opening the bowling.

I think Norman became a lot more aggressive by watching my attitude. Also Angus Fraser. He was very talented but at first he lacked the I'm-gonna-get-you aggression that you need. Those guys observed the way I went about things and maybe the mental side of my game rubbed off on them.

I enjoyed my time at Middlesex so much. When I first arrived I was a young Bajan boy away from home with no friends or family in England. It was such a warm place. Even the girls in the office were like: "Oh Wayne, you're back, come in and see us!" Or if I was overseas I'd get a call: "Wayne, when are you coming back? Your sweaters are here waiting for you!" The welcome was always so warm.

All the guys were so friendly. The late Mike Smith, Smudger, was terrific, really terrific. He used to clamour to pick me up and take me to the matches. He was the one who nicknamed me the 'Diamond'. If I was travelling with someone else he would say to them: "You've gotta take care of the Diamond – make sure he gets there in one piece."

It was very disappointing when I started to pick up injuries. Early in the '88 season Norman Cowans bowled a long half-volley to someone – how dare he do that! I chased it to the boundary and my back went as I picked it up. Then my Achilles went against Yorkshire. My body was telling me something. ●

BY JOHN STERN

FIGHT AND FLIGHT

Left-arm and right-arm, attack and defence, Cambridge University and the school of hard knocks – **Phil Edmonds** and **John Emburey**, formed the perfect partnership

Phil Edmonds is sitting on the edge of a large desk in his Mayfair office. Maps of Sudan adorn the walls. He is wearing a Middlesex tie: a sartorial toss-up, he explains, between that and a John Emburey benefit tie. Edmonds is an elusive character – it was ever thus – spending much of his time in various parts of Africa attending to his business interests. But over the course of an evening he speaks – though preferring not to be interviewed on the record – with great affection, if at times hazy recollection, of a county career that was outstanding by any measure, even if it is tinged with a sense of frustration because of the obvious extent of his talent.

He speaks affectionately of team-mates, none more so than his spin twin Emburey, with whom he developed a magical, masterly and complementary double-act for a decade from the mid-1970s. Edmonds reckons Embers has been seriously under-rated and would have harvested plenty more than his 147 Test wickets had DRS been around to assist.

"We became mates, purely because of the relationship we had on the field," says Emburey, dapper in blazer and tie, perched on a bar stool in the Lord's Tavern. "We developed a partnership and Philippe was my best man in 1980. But Frances [Edmonds] got up and gave most of the speech. That's how she was. I think he fumbled around a bit so she said, 'Oh Philippe sit down' and gave the speech herself."

Of the two, Edmonds, a left-armer with the high classical action, emerged first, coming down from Cambridge University bubbling with "colonial arrogance", as he puts it, a legacy of his Zambian origins. Cricket was a pursuit, rather than a job, and his interest in playing county cricket was really a point-proving exercise, a means of fulfilling potential. That he played so long (16 years) was down to the "staccato" nature of his career. "When I considered who to sign for," Edmonds said in *A Singular Man*, his biography by Simon Barnes, "I had in my mind's eye the big press box above the Warner Stand. It would

be far easier to play for England by doing well at Lord's than it would be doing well miles away in Glamorgan." Glamorgan, Warwickshire and Leicestershire had all wanted him.

Emburey, the Peckham-born off-spinner, was with Surrey and hoped for a contract in 1971 but their spin stocks were full. He was advised by the coach Arthur McIntyre to contact Don Bennett at Middlesex. "I didn't bother because I was Surrey through and through," says Emburey. But a letter came from Bennett anyway inviting him for a trial and a three-month contract soon followed.

Because Fred Titmus was still part of the Middlesex furniture it was a long apprenticeship for Emburey and it wasn't until 1976 that Titmus was dropped for Emburey. Mike Brearley, the captain, remembers it as a "painful and difficult" moment. It was painful for all concerned because Middlesex contrived to lose the game at Dartford despite making Kent follow on. "It probably put pressure on me to perform – and I didn't!" says Emburey. Titmus returned for the next match.

This was a momentous Championship-winning season for Middlesex but Emburey was at a crossroads. "I was coming up 24 and at the end of '76 I was thinking of giving up cricket because there didn't seem to be an opportunity for me. Then Fred retired at the end of the year and I signed a contract."

Edmonds, who was one of four Middlesex bowlers to take more than 70 wickets in 1976, had already played for England at this point. But his international career would be sporadic, a fate that was intertwined with his turbulent relationship with Brearley, who captained England in the late 1970s and again in 1981.

On pages 30-39 Brearley explains the complex and changing nature of their relationship from his perspective. Emburey believes that Edmonds, a talented batsman himself who opened for a time, began to resent the pace of Brearley's batting "which was very slow at times". In the days when the first innings of County Championship matches were restricted to 100 overs per

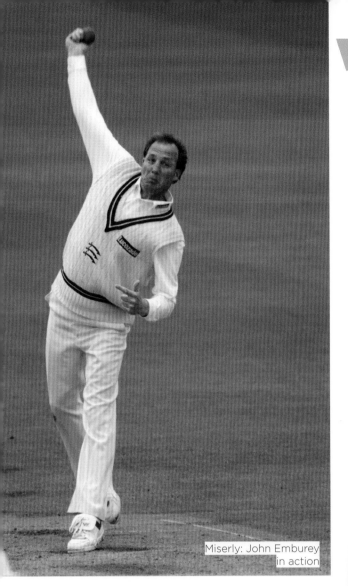

Miserly: John Emburey in action

> **We became mates and Philippe was my best man in 1980. But his wife gave most of the speech**

when he was 12th man. "We were 121 for 3, chasing 202, and a bit nervous. Here was Phil, a Test player in his own right, going round telling everyone that it would be fine and to stay relaxed. I thought that was fabulous and showed an interesting aspect of his character."

Edmonds had been vice-captain and hoped for the ultimate honour but, says Gatting, "people weren't sure Philippe was the right man, especially Brears". Emburey became vice-captain after the 1981 season but then was replaced later that winter by Gatting because of his participation in the rebel tour to South Africa.

Feeling somewhat under-appreciated, Edmonds's bowling declined to a point where his run-up comprised only a pace or two and he struggled to land the ball effectively. He recovered spectacularly to have a career-best season in 1984 when he took 77 wickets and made his highest score, 142 against Glamorgan at Swansea in an innings when no other player made 50.

Classical action: Phil Edmonds twirling away

side, Edmonds would often be required for some pre-declaration, lower-order bashing.

But Edmonds was also bright, a contrarian and an individualist. "If you said it was white he would say it was black," says Mike Gatting, who took over the Middlesex captaincy in 1983 after Brearley's retirement. "He'd always been a member of the awkward squad, albeit in a very endearing way," says Tim Lamb, former seam bowler and Edmonds's room-mate on away trips. Lamb recalls being woken up at 6am by the *Today* programme on the radio. Edmonds's own recollection is actually that he used to prefer to sleep with the radio on all night because he didn't like silence.

On the flip side, Vince van der Bijl recalls a different side of Edmonds in the 1980 Gillette Cup final against Surrey

PHILIPPE-HENRI EDMONDS

Born: March 8, 1951, Lusaka, Zambia
Left-arm orthodox spin bowler, right-hand batsman,

- 883 first-class wickets (1,246 overall) at 23.55 for Middlesex 1971–92
- 5,036 first-class runs (7,650 overall) at 19.82 for Middlesex, 2 hundreds
- 125 wickets at 34.18 in 51 Tests; 875 runs at 17.50
- 284 one-day wickets for Middlesex
- Topped county averages in 1973 (30 wickets at 17.83)
- Four seasons with more than 70 Championship wickets (best 77 at 26.37 in 1984)
- Five County Championship titles
- Five one-day trophies
- Middlesex cap 1974
- Middlesex benefit 1983

JOHN ERNEST EMBUREY

Born: August 20, 1952, Peckham
Right-arm off-spin bowler, right-hand batsman

- 1,250 first-class wickets (1,608 overall) for Middlesex at 24.09 1975–95
- 147 wickets at 38.40 in 64 Tests
- 9,053 first-class runs (12,021 overall) at 24.40, 7 hundreds, for Middlesex
- 491 one-day wickets, 3,043 runs for Middlesex
- Seven County Championship titles
- Eight one-day trophies
- Man of the match in 1986 Benson and Hedges Cup final
- Middlesex cap 1977
- Wisden Cricketer of the Year 1984
- Middlesex benefit 1986, 1995 (testimonial)
- England captain 1988
- Also played for Northamptonshire

He and Emburey extended their county partnership to the international stage and performed to great effect in the Ashes victories of 1985 and 1986-87. Was there ever competition between the two? "Probably there was," says Emburey. "I'm sure that we both wanted to get more wickets than each other. And more often than not we were competing for a spot in the England side. But we were chalk and cheese in terms of the way we bowled. Look at our records and they're very similar. It just goes to show that there's more than one way to skin a cat."

"He was a bit like Fred [Titmus] in some ways," Brearley says of Emburey. "They both liked to have two fielders for the price of one. You'd want your man deep enough to stop the boundary but close enough to stop the single. John was an exceptionally canny and shrewd all-round cricketer."

Gatting says: "Embers was always miserly, which was maybe a Titmus thing – or maybe just a Surrey thing. Philippe wanted to be more attacking, more flamboyant. He wanted to rip it, for it to pitch leg and hit off."

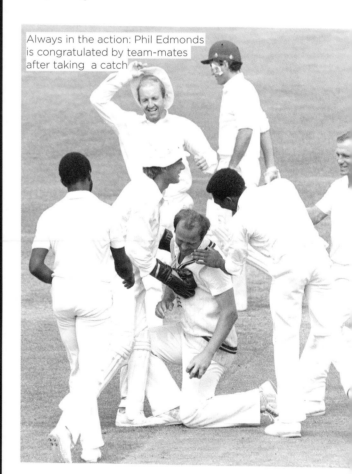

Always in the action: Phil Edmonds is congratulated by team-mates after taking a catch

" Philippe was hard work at times but his desire not to come second was amazing

On the accusation of Edmonds being too attacking, Simon Barnes wrote in *A Singular Man*: "For Edmonds, these duels are not grim, vicious, grinding struggles. They are flamboyant explosions of single combat: Captain Blood on the beach with whirling rapier and have-at-you-now. He bowls as a D'Artagnan of cricket. Mentally he is always ready to swing across the room on a chandelier."

John Carr was one of Middlesex's finest close fielders in the late '80s and early '90s: "It was amazing to see how they would pin batsmen to the crease. They were big men and strong men in their own ways. The pace and bounce they used to get meant batsmen were rabbits in the headlights. It was in a different way to, say, Wayne Daniel but almost equally as intimidating."

Gatting adds: "You knew where you were with Philippe and I was always grateful for that. He was hard work at times but his desire on the pitch not to come second was amazing. You knew when he got the ball in his hand that unless he was trying to prove a point – which he generally was – he was a magnificent bowler."

On the subject of proving points, Gatting recalls an exchange of views about field placings: "It was turning square and I suggested having a short leg rather than a midwicket. Philippe said: 'No, no.' So I went to backward short leg and the next two balls were full bungers that were smashed through midwicket. 'There I told you so'. You always ended up swearing at him.

"He always wanted to be in the action. Normally you put a youngster in at short leg but Philippe wanted to go there. 'I want to look in their [the batsmen's] eyes,' he'd say when Wayne Daniel was bowling. In the end he decided it wasn't really the place to be and he went back to slip or gully."

Edmonds's career with Middlesex ended in 1987 but only after a typically unconventional request to his old mate Tim Lamb, who was now the secretary of the club, to continue playing for the county as an amateur. "One of his requests," recalls John Carr, "was that he be able to take important phone calls at third man or fine leg to carry on his business interests while spinning teams out."

Lamb remembers: "He wanted to loosen the shackles and be more his own man and pursue other income-generating opportunities. I told him I would have to consult with my committee colleagues but we all agreed it would be unworkable. Not paying him would make it harder to exercise any sort of control over his activities. So I arranged a meeting with Phil to discuss it. This wasn't a meeting I was particularly looking forward to. I went through all the reasons of why his grand plan to roll back the years to the Gentlemen and Players era was unworkable. I expected him to round on me but he just said: 'Oh well, worth a try' and walked out." And that, apart from a one-off comeback at Trent Bridge in 1992 when he answered an injury crisis SOS by arriving in a Rolls-Royce, was that.

Emburey, though, kept twirling along. The side-effect of a second rebel tour to South Africa was his greater availability for Middlesex. He formed a new partnership with another mercurial left-armer, Phil Tufnell, and continued to help deliver success to his adopted county with further Championship titles won in 1990 and 1993. In fact he seemed to get better with age. He took his career-best figures a month before his 41st birthday: 8 for 40 and 12 wickets in the match against Hampshire on the way to the 1993 pennant. He averaged 52 with the bat that year as well, the culmination of a career-long metamorphosis from shot-less tail-ender to highly effective, if idiosyncratic, No.7 batsman.

He finished aged 43 in 1995, having taken 74 Championship wickets and also played a Test against West Indies. He had been Middlesex's leading wicket-taker in each of his last four seasons. "I could have carried on until I was 50 – comfortably," he says. He wasn't far off – his last first-class match was in June 1997 for Northamptonshire, whom he joined as player-coach. He still plays league cricket for Totteridge Millhillians and he's still moaning about the slope on their ground: "Massive, much bigger than Lord's – it's bloody difficult." Meanwhile Philippe-Henri checks the share prices. ●

THE LION AND THE ROSE

DESMOND HAYNES
Middlesex & West Indies
Photo: PAUL LEWIS

Rob Steen profiles Middlesex's other favourite Bajan, **Desmond Haynes**, whose contribution extended beyond just racking up the runs

The secret to success according to Desmond Leo Haynes, junior half of the most prolific opening firm in Test history and senior partner of a highly productive one with Mike Roseberry for Middlesex, lay in balancing passion with restraint. "I keep telling Mickey Roseberry that he has to make love to the ball instead of raping it," he told his opening partner. Mind you, if the Lion of Barbados never quite mustered the courage to issue the same advice to Gordon Greenidge, who always drove and cut as if punishing the poor ball for every racist slight he had suffered growing up in Reading, you could hardly blame him.

Desi met Mickey in 1989. England victories were scarcer than proponents of the Berlin Wall and imports were getting a bashing. In that year's *Cricketers' Who's Who*, Roseberry himself had insisted that the situation had "got well out of hand". Three years and one England A call-up later, he was whistling a more gracious tune.

"Before Desi came I had the impression that not all overseas players performed as they should. You could bring in three or four English players for [their] salaries. And they didn't help with coaching. Then Desi arrived and made me alter all those preconceptions. He [was] very helpful to me and wonderful in the dressing room. Even before you met him you always had this indelible impression of that big, wonderful smile and that bubbly manner. He really is like that. He really is a noble, happy character."

Back then the Middlesex dressing room was the most cosmopolitan in the land. Desi, indeed, felt comfortable enough, according to Roseberry, to refer himself by the N-word. Roseberry and co preferred 'Budgie' – oy, what a natterer he was. "Live, Love, Laugh" declared the pendant that hung around that substantial neck – the mantra of a man who had come a mighty long way from his roots.

Raising him had been a struggle for Arletha, a single mother running a two-room household in Holders Hill serving a dozen people, bereft of electricity and running water: "Desi had a big head. We used to send him up the hill with a bucket on it." Her eyes welled up with pride and gratitude as she told me how, after joining Kerry Packer's revolution, the eldest of her three sons did all he could for her as well as the siblings, aunts, uncles and cousins who constituted the 14-strong "family circle".

"Desi was all I had to depend on when I got the sack. He helped all the members of the family circle. I took sick, got told it was cancer, so he bought me a home, furnished it too. Then he [set me up with] a shop." Yet even though the Caribbean public at large was by no means unsympathetic to the Packer defectors, plenty accused Desi of treason: "What he had to put up with, all those nasty words, was terrible."

Happily for Middlesex, a more measured collection of words transformed Desi's outlook during the winter before he became a Seaxe. "I was staying with some friends in Sydney [and] casually picked up a book on psychology. It told me it was better to visualise good days. It instilled a sense of the positive. I'd never been a worrier, but I was always seeking to protect what I had, what I'd earned, always scared of losing it all.

"For the first time, I began to set myself goals. The main one was to make a [Test] century in Australia – in Holders Hill the general view was that if you don't score runs there you can't bat. During practice for the Perth Test I walked back from the nets to the dressing room with my bat raised as if I'd just made that hundred. I visualised it, then I lived it."

That positivism infected his new county confrères – Roseberry above all. "At one stage I got out hooking three

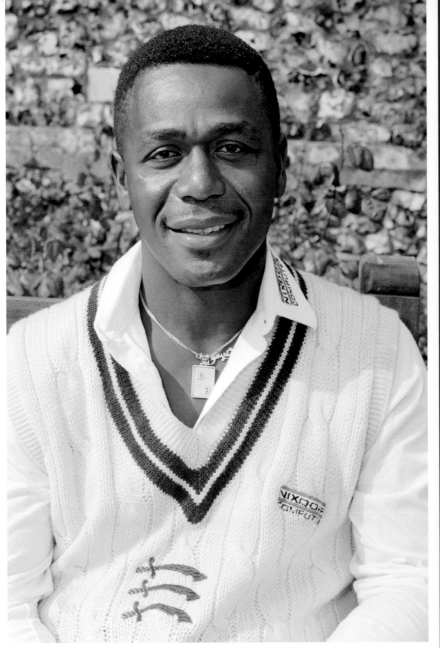

DESMOND LEO HAYNES
Born: February 15, 1956, Holders Hill, Barbados
Right-hand batsman

- 7,071 first-class runs (26,030 overall) at
  49.10, 21 hundreds, for Middlesex 1989–94
- 7,487 runs at 42.29, 18 hundreds, in 116
  Tests for West Indies
- 4,105 one-days runs at 48.86 for Middlesex
- Middlesex's leading Championship run-scorer
  in 1989 and 1990 (2,036 runs at 63.62)
- County's leading one-day batsman in 1990
  (1,353 runs at 61.50, almost 500 more than
  the next man, Mark Ramprakash)
- County Championship titles 1990 and 1993
- Sunday League title 1992 – tournament's
  leading run-scorer (839 runs at 69.91)
- Middlesex cap 1989
- Wisden Cricketer of the Year 1991

> **"** He said if I didn't get on the England
> A tour he would streak round Lord's.
> Lord's, thankfully, was spared

times in four innings, which should never happen at Uxbridge, so I asked Desi what I should do. He told me to carry on because hooking was generally a good earner for me. I shouldn't lose faith. In 1992 he said that if I didn't get on the A tour he would strip off and streak round Lord's. Lord's, thankfully, was spared."

Desi thanks God for a good many things – "that I never fell into bad company, that I was treated so well at Middlesex and, perhaps most of all, that I experienced the camaraderie of the game". The game thanks him for all that nobility and laughter – and for making love to that ball. ●

Rob Steen, who has been a Middlesex follower since 1967 and reported on them for more than 20 years, is the author of Desmond Haynes: Lion of Barbados

INTERVIEW BY JOHN STERN

"DON'T WORRY LAD, YOU'LL PROBABLY END UP WITH A FIVE-FOR"

Richard Johnson relives the day in 1994 when as a teenager with a swollen knee he made bowling history

Middlesex's visit to Derby in August 2013 was a trip down a gloriously unforgettable memory lane for the bowling coach, Richard Johnson, who, 19 years earlier and still only 19 himself, had become the fifth Middlesex bowler to take all ten wickets in a first-class innings.

There were other connections. His coaching colleague Mark Ramprakash had been the man who took the vital, final catch to deliver Johnson his rare figures. In addition one of the umpires in the 2013 match, Peter Willey, had also been standing in 1994 and it was his throwaway remark that stuck in Johnson's mind.

It had been a good pitch. Kim Barnett made a century in Derbyshire's first innings of 344. Three Middlesex batsmen made hundreds in reply and despite a collapse from 433 for 3 to 545 all out they still had a lead of 201.

On a hot, humid afternoon Johnson, in only his ninth County Championship match, took the new ball once more. "I was due to have the first of many knee ops in a couple of weeks and I was struggling – it kept swelling up," Johnson remembers. "I bowled one of the stiffest opening overs I've ever bowled in my life. I felt awful. My first ball was a wide long-hop that was cut for four by Barnett. The fifth ball was another awful long-hop that was cut straight to Embers at backward point. I took my cap at the end of the over from Peter Willey and said: 'Pete, it's going to be one of those days – my body won't move, I feel stiff and tired.' He said: 'Don't worry lad, you'll probably end up with a five-for.'"

At tea Derbyshire were 43 for 7, their batting described as "reckless" and "embarrasingly inept" in their own yearbook. Johnson, dodgy right knee and all, had 7 for 22 from 12 unbroken overs. "I sat at tea with an ice pack on my knee and

was struggling. Kevin Shine came up and said: 'You have to bowl – how many times are you going to have a chance to get all ten?' That was probably the first time I'd thought about it. I got a wicket quite early after tea and that kept me going."

When the ninth went down, Mike Gatting replaced the medium pace of Mark Feltham with the occasional off spin of Desmond Haynes. "Felts wasn't happy," says Johnson, "because it was the first time that he had been taken off *in case* he gets a wicket." Haynes bowled two maidens, though, says John Carr: "I'm not sure he entirely joined in the party spirit of not trying to get a wicket."

Devon Malcolm was the last man in. "I thought 'well, if I don't do it now I'm never going to,'" says Johnson. "I bowled the perfect yorker but he dug it out, got a single up the other end and I never bowled another ball to him. I ended up getting the other bloke."

That other bloke was left-arm spinner Matthew Taylor who, in only his second Championship match, had been taken apart by Gatting in Middlesex's innings. Meanwhile at mid-on Middlesex's left-arm spinner was having a memory lapse. "I suddenly realised that I didn't know his first name – I just knew him as Johnno," recalls Phil Tufnell. "If he was about to get a ten-for I thought I'd better find out!"

"It was the best ball I bowled all day – good length, nipped away and bounced," says Johnson. It went to straight to Ramprakash who had just been brought in to the slip cordon. "Ramps told me afterwards that as he walked in there he knew the next ball was coming to him," says Johnson. "He said it was the weirdest feeling he'd ever had on the field."

DLESEX MAXIMUMS

5 – Teddy Walker 10 for 104 v Lancashire.
d Trafford, July 20, 21, 22. Lancashire 243 and 178
owley 60; VE Walker 44.2-5 104-10); Middlesex
RD Walker 84, AJA Wilkinson 59) and 116 (R
on 5-45). Lancashire won by 62 runs.

3 – George Burton 10 for 59 v Surrey.
e Oval, July 19, 20, 21. Middlesex 161 (SW Scott
Beaumont 4-31) and 53 (G Lohmann 7-32); Surrey
KJ Key 51; G Burton 52.3-25-59-10) and 52-7.
y won by 3 wickets.

0 – Albert Trott 10-42 v Somerset.
unton, August 6, 7, 8. Somerset 89 (AE Trott 14.2-
-10) and 327 (LCH Palairet 92, CA Bernard 72, E
on 50); Middlesex 139 (B Cranfield 7-74) and 280-
Warner 84, Trott 34*; Cranfield 4-106). Middlesex
y 1 wicket.

9 – Gubby Allen 10-40 v Lancashire.
rd's, June 15, 17, 18. Lancashire 241 (GE Tyldesley
GOB Allen 25.3-10-40-10) and 310-9 dec. (JL
ood 106*, RK Tyldesley 53); Middlesex 228 (HW Lee
RK Tyldesley 5-40, EA McDonald 4-108) and 170-5
.05*). Match drawn.

aptain Nigel Haig was particularly keen for the
eur Gubby Allen to appear in this fixture against
de who had won been county champions for the
ous three seasons. But Allen explained he could
e there for the start of the first day because he
o work at Debenhams. He arrived 20 minutes after
art of play and took a wicket immediately to leave
ashire 90 for 1 at lunch. At tea they were 215 for
en completed the innings with four wickets in five
including the stumping of Ted McDonald. He had
hit on the thigh and then come down the pitch to the
pall. Allen bowled a slow, wide delivery that allowed
etkeeper Fred Price to get up to the stumps. Having
the first 'all ten' at Lord's since 1906, Allen, having
ed eight of his victims bowled, grabbed his sweater
an from the field. *The Times* remarked on "the great
at which he made the ball leave the pitch and
d: "It was in fact a truly exhilarating exhibition of
powling – real fast bowling at its best." **JS**

RICHARD LEONARD JOHNSON

Born: December 29, 1974, Chertsey
Right-arm fast-medium bowler, right-
hand batsman

- 279 first-class wickets (528 overall) at
  28.46 for Middlesex 1992–2000, 2007
- Middlesex cap 1995
- Took 6 for 33 in first of three Tests v
  Zimbabwe 2003
- Also played for Somerset 2001–06

SCORECARD

COUNTY CHAMPIONSHIP
DERBYSHIRE V MIDDLESEX AT DERBY, JUNE 30, JULY 1, 2, 1994

Toss: Derbyshire. Result: Middlesex won by an innings and 96 runs.

Derbyshire 344 (KJ Barnett 148, AS Rollins 53*; MA Feltham 5-69);
Middlesex 545 (MW Gatting 147, MR Ramprakash 131, JD Carr 108*, Extras 81; CM Wells 4-52)

DERBYSHIRE	2ND INNINGS	R
KJ Barnett	c Emburey b Johnson	4
MJ Vandrau	b Johnson	0
TJG O'Gorman	c Emburey b Johnson	18
CJ Adams	c Carr b Johnson	8
DG Cork	c Feltham b Johnson	4
†AS Rollins	c and b Johnson	2
CM Wells	b Johnson	32
AE Warner	c Brown b Johnson	2
SJ Base	lbw b Johnson	20
M Taylor	c Ramprakash b Johnson	5
DE Malcolm	not out	1
Extras	(2 b, 4 lb, 2 nb, 1 w)	9
Total	**(all out, 40.5 overs)**	**105**

Fall of wickets: 1-4, 2-9, 3-30, 4-34, 5-35, 6-36, 7-43, 8-93, 9-104

MIDDLESEX	O	M	R	W
Johnson	18.5	6	45	10
Shine	6	2	15	0
Feltham	12	4	37	0
Tufnell	2	1	2	0
Haynes	2	2	0	0

Umpires: R Palmer, P Willey

Johnson had become the first bowler
to take all ten in England since 1964.
What next? "Pandemonium. Alan Moss
bought champagne for the changing
room and then we had a night out." As
well as Johnson's achievement they could
celebrate their second successive innings
victory in the Championship.

"But it's a funny achievement," says
Johnson. "It didn't really mean that much
at the time and it's only as I've got older
that I realise how much of an achievement
it is. There's a lot of luck involved. It's as
much about other bowlers not taking
wickets as it is about you taking them." ●

INTERVIEW BY JOHN STERN

BUCK UP FOR THE CUP

Chris Rogers reflects on his own remarkable year and assesses the current state of the team

The selection of four-day captain Chris Rogers for Australia's 2013 Ashes squad brought mixed emotions for Middlesex followers. But the worrying prospect of being without their leading batsman for a decent chunk of the Championship season was quickly mitigated by pride and feelings of goodwill towards a man who has proved such a worthy ambassador for the club on and off the field. Those feelings only grew when 'Buck' reached an emotional maiden Test hundred in the fourth Test at Durham.

Joining Middlesex in 2011 after spells at Leicestershire, Northamptonshire and Derbyshire, Rogers made an immediate impact. He scored 1,286 Championship runs at 58.45 – 401 more than the next leading run-scorer, Sam Robson – to help gain promotion from Division Two. He took over the four-day captaincy from Neil Dexter briefly at the end of 2011 and then more permanently early in 2012. He has continued to churn out the runs at the top of the order. His combined record in 2012 and 2013 was 2,154 Championship runs at 46.82 and only in 2013 did he cede the leading run-scorer's spot to his Sydney-born protégé Robson.

What attracted you to Middlesex?
It wasn't a hard decision. Middlesex is a big club and I saw a lot of potential when I played against them for Derbyshire. The lure of living in London and playing at Lord's was a great combination and an opportunity that I thought wasn't going to come along again. It's an amazing club with an amazing history and you have to respect that. With that comes a lot of expectation but that's also one of the things I like about it here.

What sort of progress have the county made since you arrived?
We've done well in many respects. It was excellent to get promoted and then to finish third in 2012. People shouldn't under-estimate how good an achievement that was and how tough a competition it is. There's a good feeling at the club right now and I think it's in a very healthy position.

There seems to be a spirit of togetherness …
Yeah. First and foremost you have to give Angus Fraser a lot of credit for that. He is as good a person as I've met in cricket. Honest as the day is long but intelligent, perceptive and shrewd. He has had to make tough decisions but they have all been for the betterment of the club. He has also made a lot of good appointments such as Richard Scott, Richard Johnson and most recently Mark Ramprakash. All-round good people who have the best interests of the club at heart.

How have you found the captaincy?
I really enjoy it now. I've grown into it. I'd been captain at Derby but there were a few issues because it wasn't a particularly successful club. To come here and captain a big club with all the history and reputation is a huge honour. Having such good people around and us doing well makes it even better. I guess Dexy might want it back at some stage but I'm really enjoying it and I think the guys respond pretty well to me so hopefully I can do it a while longer.

How would you assess the 2013 season?
In some respects it was a good consolidation year. We've played some good cricket again and beat the best sides which is a good

CHRISTOPHER JOHN LLEWELLYN ROGERS
Born: August 31, 1977, Kogarah, Sydney
Left-hand batsman

- 3,479 first-class runs (20,498 overall) at
  48.31 for Middlesex 2011–13, 10 hundreds
- 386 runs at 35.09 in 6 Tests for Australia
  including five Tests and maiden hundred in
  2013 Ashes
- Has scored at least 1,100 runs in each of his
  three Middlesex seasons
- Middlesex cap 2011
- Middlesex four-day captain from mid-2011,
  leading county to Championship promotion
- Also played for Leicestershire,
  Northamptonshire and Derbyshire
- Currently with Victoria in Sheffield Shield,
  previously Western Australia

STEVEN THOMAS FINN
Born: April 4, 1989, Watford
Right-arm fast bowler, right-hand batsman

- 209 first-class wickets (326 overall) for
  Middlesex at 26.75 2009–13
- 54 one-day wickets (119 overall) for Middlesex
- 90 wickets in 23 Tests at 29.40; 59 ODI
  wickets; 25 T20 international wickets
- Took 9-61 (14 in match) v Worcestershire 2010
- Middlesex cap 2009
- ICC Emerging Player of the Year 2010

LEADING PERFORMERS OF 2013
Championship run-scorer
SD Robson 1,180 runs at 47.20
Championship wicket-taker
TJ Murtagh 60 wickets at 20.40
One-day run-scorer
DJ Malan 552 runs at 69.00
One-day wicket-taker
TS Roland-Jones 18 wickets at 22.88
Twenty20 run-scorer
DJ Malan 351 runs at 39.00
Twenty20 wicket-taker
KD Mills 11 wickets at 26.45

> ## " There's a lot of expectation but that's
> one of the things I like about it here

sign but we were hoping to be right in the mix for the Championship and we fell away so that was disappointing.

Our batting didn't stand up when we needed it to towards the end of the season. And we were a little bit flat at times. If you want to win you have to be ruthless. There's big room for improvement, particularly in the middle order. That's the challenge for us in the future – we all need to contribute. The difference between Durham and other sides was that they had 11 contributors and most others are lucky to have seven or eight.

Ollie Rayner got 41 wickets and that was great for us. We've invested heavily in our seam department so for the spinners to win a game for us at The Oval was excellent. There's still a long way to go for Ollie and Ravi Patel and you can't rest on one or two good performances but there are signs that we might have the spin area covered.

How did you find returning to the county side after the Ashes?
I found it exceptionally difficult

coming back into the side and I didn't really understand how hard it was going to be. And in that Somerset game, having only had two days' break, I was a bit nowhere. I still wanted to do well for Middlesex but it's hard to focus and find motivation when you have invested so much of yourself into something else. But it was also a good learning curve for me. I still have a real desire to see Middlesex succeed and for that to happen I'm going to have to come back from playing higher honours.

MATES' RATES

England fast bowler **Steven Finn** on how the Middlesex dressing room keeps him grounded

You're a local lad so was Middlesex always on your radar?
When I was real young I just played cricket and loved it but always used to keep an eye on what Middlesex were doing. One of the first games I watched was a one-day game at Southgate against Yorkshire when Glenn McGrath was playing – I remember that very fondly. Being associated with Middlesex was very prestigious so when I was 13 and asked to join the Academy it was just a massive honour. I'm very grateful to all the people who have put in so much work on my behalf since then.

There seems to be a very good spirit within the club now – would you agree?
The dressing room is very close knit. The fact that everyone gets on together and are mates helps a lot with team cohesion and makes a big difference when you go out there and pull the whites on. A lot of that is down to Gus and the people he's brought into the club.

How easy do you find it to fit back into the group when you've been away playing for England?
Very easy. I keep in contact with the Middlesex guys all the time. They always keep my feet on the ground but they're always they're for me if times are hard. Last summer was quite difficult for me, being in and out of the team and watching a lot of cricket. When I've come back to Middlesex I've thoroughly enjoyed it and hopefully that's helping me get back to my best. I'm very grateful to everyone at the club but in particular my team-mates.

What are your Middlesex career highlights so far?
Getting nine-for at Worcester was special, obviously, and one of my first memories of being involved with the playing staff was being promoted in the Pro40 in 2009. The Twenty20 Cup was a big highlight and likewise promotion to the first division of the Championship in 2011. To hold our own in the first division with basically the same group of players has been a great effort. We knew that a club like Middlesex belonged in the first division but it's no good saying it if you don't do something about it. It was important we got back there and hopefully now that we have the right team ethos we can stay there.

What stands out for you in that promotion year?
I didn't play in that many games but I do remember the way we got ourselves out of tricky situations more often than not. In the home game against Surrey Neil Dexter and John Simpson batted us out of trouble and into a winning position [a stand of 254 for the first-innings fifth wicket]. And then the bowlers would come up trumps just when we were under the pump and looking at a first-innings deficit. It's things like that that get you promoted.

How did you enjoy playing against Chris Rogers for a change in the Ashes?
He's a fantastic player and fully deserved his Test call-up. I was very pleased for him. It was a bit different to pull on the shirt to play against him. It was almost the perfect scenario – he got a hundred but they didn't win a game and we still won the Ashes. ●

THE NEXT GENERATION

Middlesex have always been at the forefront of youth development, writes **Alan Coleman**

Thirty years of development: Middlesex U13 in 1982 (including Mark Ramprakash in the background) ...

Middlesex has an illustrious history of youth cricket in the county, and has always been seen as a front-runner in youth development, with representative teams playing as early as the 1960s.

The Middlesex Colts Association was formed in 1966 as a governing body of youth club cricket, and its first representative sides appeared in 1968 at under-16 and under-18 level. The Schools Cricket Association of Middlesex was simultaneously running representative teams at this point, with an extensive fixture list for select boys who had performed well in schools cricket.

In the early 1970s, Middlesex stalwart Jack Robertson helped to introduce a formalised coaching programme for the best under-11 players, one of the first at county level in the country. By 1975, Ted Jackson's vision led to the introduction of an under-13 team overseen by David Green, and this was followed with the introduction of under-15 and under-17 teams the year after, under the title of the Middlesex Youth Coaching Scheme.

Seeing the value of high-level coaching for young players, Middlesex lent a financial hand to youth cricket by funding the coaching programme from 1976 and the matches from 1986. The club further cemented the importance of youth cricket by inviting both Jackson and Green on to the main club committee, with county coach Don Bennett a familiar figure at training sessions for all ages during this time.

After its first 24 years, the Middlesex youth programme had generated 52 first-class cricketers. By 1996, the schools association and the youth sub-committee had merged their individual programmes, creating a wide-ranging and challenging coaching and match programme for the best young players from all areas of Middlesex.

Tours have been a major part of Middlesex youth cricket from the start, with the under-13s still travelling to the Midlands as they did in the 1970s. In addition, the under-11s have been regular visitors to the west country during this period, and many of the county's former first-team players came through the Cambridge Under-19 Festival, which is no longer held.

In 2003, the Middlesex Academy was launched under Toby Radford, its first director, with the goal of helping the county's most

... and the U10s in 2012

> **After its first 24 years, the Middlesex youth programme had generated 52 first-class cricketers**

talented young players reach the professional game. As we reach our 150th year, 15 players have graduated on to a county professional staff, with Steven Finn the first from the Academy to represent England in Test, one-day international and Twenty20 cricket.

In our 150th year Middlesex CCC will be represented by 11 youth teams, with over 150 boys and girls aged from 11 to 19 years old, wearing the famous Seaxes in games against other counties. ●

For more information on youth cricket in Middlesex please visit: **www.middlesexccc.com**

Alan Coleman, who played four one-day matches for Middlesex in 2001–02, is the county's head of youth cricket

BY JOHN STERN

RAD OF IRON

Between 1977 and 1988 Middlesex won six one-day finals at Lord's. **Clive Radley**, the club's current president, played in five of them and was man of the match in three

The mental image is indelible. A dab down to third man is followed by a feverishly scampered single, probably with Graham Barlow haring down from the other end, with a second run almost guaranteed. This was embryonic one-day cricket. This was Radley style.

There were nudges, nurdles, flicks and angular adjustments, all methods ingrained in our modern Twenty20 consciousness but 30 or 40 years ago, innovative and unorthodox. "I certainly had to adapt," says Radley, who first came to Middlesex from Norfolk as a 17-year-old in 1961 two years before the start of the Gillette

Cup. "I wasn't a big hitter so I really had to think about my tactics. People used to bowl fairly straight at me so I had to make my own lines and manoeuvre it around, getting inside or outside the line of the ball."

> **" I wasn't a big hitter so I really had to think about my tactics. People used to bowl fairly straight at me so I had to make my own lines**

Mike Brearley's assessment is: "Clive was shrewd. He didn't say much and it was difficult to get him to say things but when he did you listened. It was normally pragmatic and immediate. The team always felt that if he was still in we were in with a chance in tight matches. He often saw us through. Against anybody but the real quicks he would want to get a long way forward and he'd get right across his wicket and score with nudges into the leg side. And then he has got freer or in a one-day match, later in an innings, he'd give himself room and hit the ball over extra cover and through the off side. His hands would free up and it was as if there were two different players."

Radley's first one-day game for the county in 1965 was momentous. It was the first time Sussex, who had won the first two Gillette Cup tournaments, had been beaten in this new format. Middlesex made 280 for 8 in their 60 overs, a hefty one-day total in those days, thanks largely to a second-wicket stand of 126 between Bob Gale (74) and Peter Parfitt (66). Radley made 4 batting at No.9.

In 1975 Middlesex reached both one-day finals but lost them to Leicestershire and Lancashire. Both opponents were strong, canny sides. "We weren't ready to win games then," says Mike Selvey. Two years later Middlesex were back in the Gillette Cup final and this time it would be different.

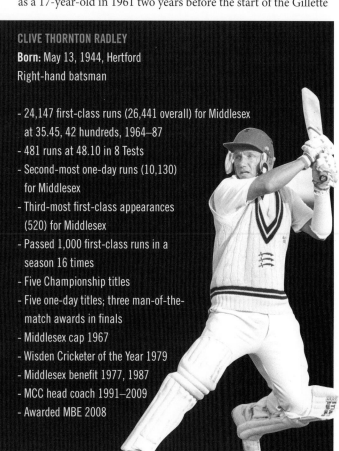

CLIVE THORNTON RADLEY
Born: May 13, 1944, Hertford
Right-hand batsman

- 24,147 first-class runs (26,441 overall) for Middlesex at 35.45, 42 hundreds, 1964–87
- 481 runs at 48.10 in 8 Tests
- Second-most one-day runs (10,130) for Middlesex
- Third-most first-class appearances (520) for Middlesex
- Passed 1,000 first-class runs in a season 16 times
- Five Championship titles
- Five one-day titles; three man-of-the-match awards in finals
- Middlesex cap 1967
- Wisden Cricketer of the Year 1979
- Middlesex benefit 1977, 1987
- MCC head coach 1991–2009
- Awarded MBE 2008

history to make such a decision and win the match. The only Glamorgan batsman to cut loose was left-hander Mike Llewellyn who wrote his name into Lord's folklore by hitting John Emburey, who was otherwise his immaculate self, on to the guttering outside the BBC commentary box at the top of the pavilion.

Norman Featherstone's off-breaks yielded three late wickets and left Middlesex with an eminently manageable target of 178. But Brearley was caught behind first ball of the innings off Malcolm Nash and then in his second over came the game-changing moment. "There's so much luck involved," says Radley. "I was shelled at second slip by Collis King, straight in. If it hadn't been for that …" Glamorgan were made to rue their miss as Radley went to make an unbeaten 85 and steer Middlesex to their first limited-overs trophy.

Celebration time. Radley says: "We started in the Tavern. There were loads of Glamorgan supporters in there and they just seemed happy they'd had a day out at Lord's."

At Lord's, September 3, 1977. Glamorgan 177-9 (60 overs) (MJ Llewellyn 62, JA Hopkins 47; NG Featherstone 3-17); Middlesex 178-5 (55.4 overs) (CT Radley 85*). Man of the match: CT Radley.

1977 – GILLETTE CUP FINAL
Middlesex beat Glamorgan by 5 wickets

Middlesex reached the final after a bizarre semi against Somerset that took six days to complete and necessitated the postponement and relocation of the County Championship match between the two sides. Middlesex comfortably won a 15-over match after putting Somerset in.

On to the final and Clive Radley already had his eyes on the prize. It was his benefit year and he cheekily asked Donald Carr, the secretary of the TCCB, whether he could assign the final as his benefit match and thereby organise a collection in the crowd, as was the tradition. He was rebuffed because it wasn't technically a Middlesex home match. So Radley offered to share the proceeds with Glamorgan's beneficiary that year, the bowler Tony Cordle, but still no joy.

There had been rain and the ground was only just fit to play. Mike Brearley won an important toss and put Glamorgan in. He would become the first captain in the competition's 15-year

1980 – GILLETTE CUP FINAL
Middlesex beat Surrey by 7 wickets

Having beaten Surrey to the Championship, Middlesex comfortably pipped their London rivals to the last 60-over competition to be sponsored by Gillette. "It's always meant a lot to beat the old enemy south of the river!" says Radley.

Vince van der Bijl was just soaking up what was for him a unique experience: "I popped into the Ladbrokes tent before it started – bear in mind we didn't have betting in South Africa – and the odds were 7/11 Middlesex and 6/1 Surrey. I certainly wasn't placing a bet but I wanted to know why the odds were so long on Surrey. The bookie said 'Brearley will always trump Knight [Surrey captain Roger Knight].'"

The bookie was spot on. After Surrey were put in, Mike Selvey (previous page) was the stand-out bowler against his former county, bowling his 12 overs straight through and finishing with 2 for 17, including five maidens. But he remembers: "My next-door neighbour taped the highlights for me and I appear once – Alan Butcher hitting me for six into the Mound Stand. I suppose the other 11.5 overs, 2 for 11 don't make for good highlights!"

Middlesex were set 203 and won with 6.1 overs to spare, Brearley playing a captain's innings. As Middlesex soaked up the acclaim of a double-winning season, van der Bijl recalls: "For two hours after the game the Surrey fans were amassed outside their changing room and serenading the team. I thought that was just amazing. Here is a team that's lost and their fans are serenading them. That was pretty special."

At Lord's, September 6, 1980. Surrey 201 (60 overs) (DM Smith 50; SP Hughes 3-60); Middlesex 202-3 (53.5 overs) (JM Brearley 96*, RO Butcher 50*). Man of the match: JM Brearley.

1983 – BENSON AND HEDGES CUP FINAL
Middlesex beat Essex by 4 runs

Clive Radley is not alone is describing this match as "the one I really remember". To Mike Gatting, the new captain, it was "an amazing game of cricket".

Having been put in, Radley single-handedly kept Middlesex's stuttering innings together: "I just kept chipping away because everyone was getting out at the other end." In his 1988 history of the club, David Lemmon says Radley's unbeaten 89 was "initially unobtrusive, ultimately commanding … As ever, he moved onto the front foot, nudging, deflecting, always dictating the length".

Chasing 197, Essex were 71 without loss after ten overs. At tea they were 113 for 1 off 25 overs and Middlesex supporters were heading for the exits. Phil Edmonds, however, got rid of the dangerous Ken McEwan and next in was the wily Essex captain

Keith Fletcher. It was time for a last throw of the dice.

"This was the big one for me," says Gatting. "Philippe said he wanted a slip, a silly mid-off and a short leg. 'You what? They want about 50 to win.' He said: 'Mate we're not going to win this by stopping runs – we need wickets." Radley continues: "I went in to bat-pad on the off side for Fletch, who was a great player of spin and had never been caught there in his life." Until now. Fletcher pushed forward to Edmonds and the ball popped up to Radley. Essex were 135 for 3, needing 61 off 23 overs.

Keith Pont was dropped and the 150 came up. But then he was hit on the head by a bouncer from Neil Williams and dropped his bat on to his stumps. "Our physio John Miller, who was blind, came out to assist Keith and we guided John out to the middle," says Radley. "John tended to Ponty and then started to help him off the field. But Ponty didn't know where he was because he'd been hit and John didn't know which direction to go in either because he was blind. So the pair of them started walking off towards the Tavern."

Derek Pringle and Stuart Turner added 29 for the sixth wicket and when Pringle was lbw to Wayne Daniel Essex needed only 12 runs from 23 balls. Time for another twist. On came 12th man John Carr to replace Williams. "I was thinking of my post-match shower and getaway from a rather sad dressing room," says Carr. "But then Stuart Turner whacked one towards me at deep mid-on. I caught it but there was a three- or four-second delay before any noise came from the crowd. It was so dark that people weren't quite sure what had happened. It was a huge relief. I remember seeing a rather pale face on the highlights!"

With only six needed and three wickets in hand, David East was caught brilliantly at mid-wicket off Cowans by Gatting, who got a hand to the ball, spun round and held the ball as it dropped behind him. In the penultimate over Ray East was run out. "He had a panic on," according to Radley who threw the wicket down brilliantly from point with one stump to aim at.

Five runs were needed from the final over but Cowans yorked Foster, and having taken three wickets in four balls, completed an astonishing win, one of the most remarkable in Middlesex's history. **JS**

BENSON AND HEDGES CUP FINAL, LORD'S, JULY 23, 1983
MIDDLESEX V ESSEX

Toss: Essex. Result: Middlesex won by 4 runs. Man of the match: CT Radley.

MIDDLESEX		Runs	Balls
GD Barlow	b Foster	14	31
WN Slack	c Gooch b Foster	1	8
CT Radley	not out	89	154
*MW Gatting	run out (Foster/DE East)	22	55
KP Tomlins	lbw b Gooch	0	1
JE Emburey	c DE East b Lever	17	44
†PR Downton	c Fletcher b Foster	10	14
PH Edmonds	b Pringle	9	18
NF Williams	c and b Pringle	13	9
WW Daniel	not out	2	3
NG Cowans	did not bat		
Extras	(3 b, 9 lb, 3 nb, 4 w)	19	
Total	(8 wickets, 55 overs)	196	

Fall of wickets: 1-10, 2-25, 3-74, 4-74, 5-123, 6-141, 7-171, 8-191

ESSEX	O	M	R	W
Lever	11	1	52	1
Foster	11	2	26	3
Pringle	11	0	54	2
Turner	11	1	24	0
Gooch	11	2	21	1

ESSEX		Runs	Balls
GA Gooch	c Downton b Williams	46	51
BR Hardie	c Downton b Cowans	49	109
KS McEwan	c Cowans b Edmonds	34	64
*KWR Fletcher	c Radley b Edmonds	3	9
KR Pont	hit wkt b Williams	7	24
DR Pringle	lbw b Daniel	16	38
S Turner	c sub (JD Carr) b Cowans	9	30
†DE East	c Gatting b Cowans	5	10
RE East	run out (Radley)	0	5
NA Foster	b Cowans	0	1
JK Lever	not out	0	1
Extras	(12 lb, 8 nb, 3 w)	23	
Total	(all out, 54.1 overs)	192	

Fall of wickets: 1-79, 2-127, 3-135, 4-151, 5-156, 6-185, 7-187, 8-191, 9-192

MIDDLESEX	O	M	R	W
Daniel	11	2	34	1
Cowans	10.1	0	39	4
Williams	11	0	45	2
Emburey	11	3	17	0
Edmonds	11	3	34	2

Umpires: HD Bird, BJ Meyer

Unbelievable!
Gatting joy as Essex collapse

BY PETER SMITH

AT THE AGE of 33 Phil Edmonds thought he had seen it all, but even he found it hard to take in cricket's latest twist as he strolled through the Lord's pavilion shortly before nine o'clock on Saturday evening.

He kept saying so.

"I just can't believe it. I just can't believe it," the Middlesex spinner muttered to himself over and over again on his walk to commiserate with Essex's stunned players.

At 21, Neil Foster had never seen anything like it before either. For him, it was a shattering experience he'll remember for years.

His walk on Saturday was pure agony, apparently unaware of the hordes of delighted Middlesex fans racing past him to catch a glimpse of a sight they thought they would never see—Mike Gatting holding aloft the Benson and Hedges Cup.

Collapse

At the end of the most amazing final in the competition's 12 years, young Foster had to be guided off the field by John Lever long after the Middlesex players had disappeared.

He was racing at the start of the final over from Norman Cowans with Essex needing five to win after yet another startling collapse brought about by panic.

One ball was all that Cowans needed. The sound was enough to tell Foster the worst when he played and missed. He stood stunned, lost in the crowd until Lever went back and steered him off.

Now the cricketing world is beginning to open up for Gatting, within two months of taking over the captaincy, as

Man-of-match Clive Radley and captain Mike Gatting with the cap they thought had got away

it never opened up even for his predecessor Mike Brearley.

Gatting has the cup which always eluded Brearley. His side is sitting handsomely on top of the championship table. And they are through to the quarter-finals of the NatWest Trophy. Cricket's first treble is on.

All this on the toss of a coin which took Middlesex through their Benson and Hedges quarter-final against Gloucestershire six weeks ago when the tie was rained off without a ball being bowled.

Operation

Everything had gone the way Essex skipper Keith Fletcher had planned at the start. He won the toss, decided to field after a stomach operation only eight days earlier which saved his life.

Then there was Foster dismissing Wilf Slack, Graham Barlow and Paul Downton as well as running out Gatting.

Essex lost their last five

wickets for seven runs off 19 deliveries to toss away victory for the second time in four days when it seemed impossible to lose.

Their dress rehearsal, the NatWest Cup match against Kent, had been a fiasco with defeat off the last ball the previous Wednesday. Saturday was a disaster after they had got within striking distance of Middlesex's 196 for eight at 135 for two only to lose by four runs.

David Graveney, Gloucester's captain, was the first person Gatting thought of once Saturday's victory champagne started to flow.

"I felt sorry for him at the time and I think of him now. I hope it works out that we play Gloucestershire in the NatWest final," said Gatting.

...with a superb return from the square-leg boundary.

Now we had things started to go wrong with the grounding of the four sharp chances. Clive Radley offered in his unbeaten 89 which gave Middlesex their fighting chance and himself the 'gold award'.

Then came Graham Gooch's dismissal after a whirlwind 46 out of Essex's first 79 runs in 18 overs and Gooch's return to the big time since being banned from Tests.

It should have been much longer.

1984 – NATWEST TROPHY FINAL
Middlesex beat Kent by 4 wickets

Cool and calm: Emburey (left) and Downton

Mike Gatting lifted his second one-day trophy in his second year of captaincy after a last-ball victory that finished in autumnal gloom at 7.45pm. Clive Radley, in his sixth final, picked up his third man-of-the-match award for an innings of 67 off 82 balls that, yet again, provided Middlesex with stability and impetus.

Chasing 233, Middlesex were 107 for 3 from 35 overs at tea, having scored only 37 from the previous 11 overs. Gatting was caught trying to pick up the pace and two overs later Chris Tavaré, the Kent captain, took off Derek Underwood when he had figures of 9-2-12-1 and three overs of his allocation left.

Paul Downton drove Underwood's replacement Richard Ellison for Middlesex's first four in 19 overs and then another. Having put on 87 for the fifth wicket Downton and Radley departed in successive overs. Now it was down to the spin twins, John Emburey and Phil Edmonds. They needed 12 off three overs, eight off two and then seven from the final over. "Fortunately we'd been in for a while and we'd adjusted to the light because the ball was coming straight to you," says Emburey. "But it was more difficult for the Kent fielders, particularly those square of the wicket."

With one ball left the scores were level and had Middlesex not scored Kent would have won because they had the higher score after 30 overs. Ellison bowled a full delivery that Emburey turned to the square-leg boundary though he describes it modestly as "a thick inside edge".

At Lord's, September 1, 1984. †Kent 232-6 (60 overs) (CS Cowdrey 58, NR Taylor 49); Middlesex 236-6 (60 overs) (CT Radley 67, PR Downton 40; KBS Jarvis 3-47). Man of the match: CT Radley.

1986 – BENSON AND HEDGES CUP FINAL
Middlesex beat Kent by 2 runs

Another tense win in the dark over Kent and another Radley masterclass though this time the 38-year-old had to concede the Gold Award to John Emburey. At lunch Middlesex were struggling on 89 for 4 from 35 overs but Radley's 54 and Emburey's late-innings 28 from 45 balls gave them a competitive total of 199 for 7.

Derek Underwood was playing in his tenth one-day final and was as usual proving hard to get away. "I had to have a dart at Deadly – it was him or us," says Radley. "I went down the wicket, took my life in my hands, hit one over mid-wicket and then two over extra cover. That gave us impetus and he snatched his sweater from the umpire. He had a habit of walking back to his

THE SUNDAY TIMES 13 JULY 1986

A self-inflicted wound is final agony for Kent

ROBIN MARLAR reports from LORD'S

WITH camera flashes showing up like bolts of lightning and batsmen telling fielders when and where to expect the ball, the 15th Benson and Hedges Cup Final was played to a 7.30 pm finish at Lord's in atrocious conditions, bad light and heavy drizzle.

Asked to bat first, Middlesex made 199 for seven off their 55 overs, setting a target of exactly 200. Needing 19 runs off the last two overs, 14 off the last, and six off the final three balls, Kent finished on 197 for eight and thus went down by two runs. For important runs, a typically mean spell of bowling and a dazzling catch from John Emburey was made man of the match.

Thus was continued the recent string of exciting finishes in cup finals at Lord's, with none more excruciating to watch than this one. Truly conditions were, on this occasion, just too bad. But the umpires consulted and let play continue for the sake of the theatre and a packed house. They were surely right, but Kent suffered agonies at the end facing the rage of Daniel.

When all is said and done, Kent brought their final agony on themselves by opting to bat second. They could have made life marginally easier had they bowled their 55 overs faster.

Middlesex owed their second-win in this competition to Clive Radley as much as anyone. Their 42-year-old senior player hit an inventive half-century. Their opening bowlers, Cowans and Daniel, still found plenty of life in the pitch and they had Kent rocky and insecure at 20 for three.

Kent were so constricted that their run-rate dropped to a little over two to an over, and it was the younger Cowdrey who brought them back into the match and set up the thrilling finish by hitting 58 with great style, the highest score of the match. Ellison, too, added much to the occasion, bowling well and batting with great bravery at the end.

In his second over Dilley, bowling fast from the Pavilion end, put one between Slack's bat and pad and bowled him off the inside edge for nought. This placed responsibility on Miller, the least experienced of the match's four left-handed openers, and guided by Gatting, the damage was repaired.

Middlesex had just raised their rate to three an over when Ellison, operating from the Nursery end, made two incisions in the 23rd over which could have been fatal for Middlesex. Off successive balls he had Gatting and Butcher caught at the wicket by the agile, active Marsh, the new Kent 'keeper. Gatting he took low down to his right, rode the edge which Butcher gave off, a pig of a first ball and then for good measure caught Miller off Cowdrey and ran out Radley as he tried from the bowler's end to entice the becalmed Emburey into a block-hole single, a gamble which Emburey declined.

Middlesex were 163 for six in the 50th over when Radley was removed, and by the end they had to thank some stout blows by Emburey and Edmonds.

If the Middlesex score looked barely adequate it would have been lower had Cowdrey and Baptiste bowled lighter; with one for 19 and three for 27 respectively, Dilley and Ellison could hardly be faulted.

Daniel soon made both of them look plain, extracting enough life out of the pitch to beat the bat with astonishing regularity. Indeed, Tavaré's bat was struck involuntarily in that opening spell of seven overs and Gatting wisely let Cowans, wayward at first, continue for nine overs, in which time he had taken two wickets and helped drive Kent far behind the clock; after 25 overs they had made only 54.

After tea, something had to be done but it was then that Emburey caught Chris Cowdrey off an intended run through the slips, soon after which Taylor was caught in the deep off Edmonds, driving front-footed.

Graham Cowdrey brought Kent back into the match by twice hitting Edmonds over the ropes in front of the Grandstand, and he and Baptiste made merry before they had to face the awesome prospect of four more overs from Daniel in well-nigh dangerous circumstances. Baptiste struck out bravely and when Graham Cowdrey was caught on the full toss Ellison gave Kent a real chance for victory.

Gatting's preference for Edmonds over Cowans proved to be a master-stroke, because Ellison was bowled. But even after that Marsh kept Kent in the hunt by smashing Hughes over square leg for six.

MIDDLESEX

W N Slack b Dilley		0
A J T Miller c Marsh		
	b C S Cowdrey	37
*Md W Gatting c Marsh b Ellison		25
R O Butcher c Marsh b Ellison		0
C T Radley run out		54
†P R Downton lbw b Ellison		13
J E Emburey b Baptiste		28
P H Edmonds not out		15
S P Hughes not out		4
EXTRAS (lb8, w11, nb4)		23
Total (7 wkts, 55 overs)		199

N G Cowans and W W Daniel did not bat.

Fall of wickets: 1-6, 2-66, 3-66, 4-88, 8-151, 6-163, 7-183.

Bowling: Dilley 11-2-19-1; Baptiste 11-0-61-1; C S Cowdrey 11-0-48-1; Ellison 11-2-27-3; Underwood 11-4-36-0.

KENT

M R Benson c Downton b Cowans		4
S G Hinks lbw b Cowans		13
G J Tavaré c Downton b Daniel		3
N R Taylor c Miller b Edmonds		19
*C S Cowdrey c Emburey		
	b Hughes	19
G R Cowdrey c Radley b Hughes		58
E A E Baptiste b Edmonds		20
R M Ellison b Edmonds		29
†S A Marsh not out		14
G R Dilley not out		4
EXTRAS (lb9, w8)		17
Total (8 wkts, 55 overs)		197

D L Underwood did not bat.

Fall of wickets: 1-17, 2-20, 3-20, 4-62, 5-72, 6-141, 7-178, 8-182.

Bowling: Cowans 9-2-18-2; Daniel 11-1-43-1; Gatting 4-0-18-0; Hughes 9-2-35-2; Emburey 11-5-16-0; Edmonds 11-1-58-3.

Umpires: D J Constant and D R Shepherd.

Swinging in vain – Ellison, destroyer of

fielding position right across a length so I used to stand on a length to stop him doing it. I literally bumped right into him. I didn't want to apologise in case he thought I was apologising for the fours. So I said 'Deadly, I've got a benefit next year – can you do a piece for my brochure?' He said: 'F*** off'. But three days later a lovely article from him dropped through my letter box."

After 35 overs Kent were 71 for 4 but recovered thanks to Graham Cowdrey's vigorous 58. His older brother Chris, the captain, had been brilliantly caught one-handed at slip by Emburey, diving away to his right. At 116 for 5 after 45 overs Wayne Daniel was brought back, the batsmen were offered the light but turned it down. With 19 needed off two overs Phil Edmonds bowled a superb over, restricting Kent to five and removing Richard Ellison.

With rain now coming down heavily, Kent needed 14 off the last over bowled by Simon Hughes. Marsh took two off the second ball and pulled the third into the Grand Stand. Six off three became five off one and Graham Dilley pulled it to the Tavern boundary but it was fielded and Middlesex had triumphed again – their tenth trophy in 11 seasons.

At Lord's, July 12, 1986. Middlesex 199-7 (55 overs) (CT Radley 54; RM Ellison 3-27); Kent 197-8 (55 overs) (GR Cowdrey 58; PH Edmonds 3-58). Man of the match: JE Emburey (28 runs and 11-5-16-0).

RED HOT RAMPBO
Glory for Gatt lads

By TED DEXTER

WORCESTER

Curtis b Fraser	4
O'Shaughnessy c Downton b Cowans	1
Hick b Fraser	4
Leatherdale b Needham	29
Neale b Hughes	64
Weston c Downton b Fraser	31
Rhodes c Emburey b Hughes	4
Newport b Hughes	4
Radford b Hughes	5
Illingworth not out	1
Dilley not out	2
Extras (lb7, w1, nb2)	10

Total (9 wkts; Inns closed) 161
Fall: 1-5, 2-9, 3-9, 4-71, 5-137, 6-140, 7-145, 8-148, 9-153.
Bowling: Cowans 12-6-23-1, Fraser 12-5-36-3, Carr 4-1-9-0, Hughes 8-0-30-4, Needham 12-1-25-1, Emburey 12-3-31-0.

MIDDLESEX

Slack b Dilley	14
Carr c Rhodes b Dilley	1
Needham b Dilley	0
Gatting run out	0
Butcher run out	24
Ramprakash c Radford b Dilley	56
Emburey b Dilley	35
Downton not out	8
Hughes not out	0
Extras (b4, lb5, w7, nb2)	18

Total (7 wkts; 55.3 overs) 162
Fall: 1-3, 2-21, 3-21, 4-25, 5-64, 6-149, 7-159.
Bowling: Dilley 12-3-29-5, Radford 11.3-3-37-0, Illingworth 12-4-24-0, Newport 10-1-20-0, Weston 2-0-9-0, Hick 5-0-19-0, O'Shaughnessy 5-0-15-0.
Middlesex won by 3 wickets.

SCARBOROUGH: Yorkshire 265-4 (Byas 111 no, Moxon 63, Robinson 60). World XI 258-9. Yorkshire won by 7 runs.

TODAY'S CRICKET — TEXACO TROPHY — (10.45) The Oval: England v Sri Lanka. FOUR COUNTIES KO COMP.— (12.00) Scarborough: Essex v Lancs. WARWICK UNDER-25 FINAL.— Edgbaston: Warwicks v Lancs.

TEENAGE prodigy Mark Ramprakash lorded it at Lord's yesterday.

"Rampbo" cracked a brilliant 56 to clinch victory by three wickets in an enthralling NatWest Trophy final.

Chasing a modest total of 161, the home team made an appalling start with Mike Gatting run out for a duck without facing a ball.

And when Graham Dilley, on release from the England team, struck with three quick wickets, Worcestershire were right on top.

The stylish 18-year-old Ramprakash went to the wicket in the 13th over of the innings when four wickets were down for only 25 and it looked a lost cause.

But nothing daunted the Hertfordshire born youngster, who played his shots as to the manor born, sharing in lucrative partnerships with old hands Roland Butcher and John Emburey.

When he became a shade anxious in the search for runs, Emburey was the calming influence and it was good to see a fresh talent suc-ceeding so gloriously at this show-piece event.

In contrast, the match was a personal disaster for star batsman Graeme Hick — clean bowled for four by a magnificent delivery from promising pace bowler Angus Fraser.

The brilliant Zimbabwian had just one chance to redeem himself with a slip catch off Emburey at a crucial point in the run chase, but that went down too.

Bowler of the day on pure figures was Graham Dilley, taking 5 for 29, but in the end the total of 161 was never quite big enough to successfully defend.

The fates appeared to have fully relented for Gatting after such an up and down season when he won the toss and engineered a dream start for Middlesex, Fraser taking two for nine in seven accurate overs.

In the end the sweet taste of victory will have washed away the memory of his personal batting tragedy which was the strangest run-out I ever saw.

Gatting seemed to be making his ground eas-ily, actually looking round to watch the ball as it followed him down the pitch.

He turned away unconcerned only to see the bails fly off from a direct hit, a sucker-punch if ever there was one.

Two others worthy of honourable mention were the ailing Phil Neale, who shored up the heart of Worcestershire's innings with a solid 64, and the Middlesex medium-pacer Simon Hughes, who brought this counter-attack to an end with a best ever return of four for 30 from eight overs.

MARK RAMPRAKASH: dashing 56

1988 – NATWEST TROPHY FINAL
Middlesex beat Worcestershire by 3 wickets

Mike Gatting was preparing to leave the pre-match practice to toss the coin with his opposite number Phil Neale when he called out to one of his players: "Oh, by the way, youngster, you're in. Enjoy the day." That youngster was Mark Ramprakash, still 18 and yet to play in the 60-over competition but picked for the final out of the blue in place of the experienced Keith Brown. "We were all flabbergasted because it came right out of left field," remembers John Emburey.

Gatting won the toss and inserted Worcestershire on a damp pitch. They were quickly 9 for 3 and 42 balls passed without a run before Graeme Hick "hit one immaculate shot for four", according to Ramprakash. But Hick was bowled through the gate by Angus Fraser (right). Neale made an innings-anchoring 64 but Worcestershire mustered only 161 for 9.

"I was floating around the dressing room wondering if I was actually going to get in," says Ramprakash. "But very quickly there was a flurry of pads coming off and on. Gatt was run out controversially without facing. He didn't think he was out. That was a thunderbolt through the dressing room. Then Slacky [Wilf Slack] dragged one on and suddenly I'm walking out to bat." Notably, the teenager was wearing his county cap rather than a helmet: "I didn't really know any different. I hadn't really worn a helmet much before and felt more comfortable in my cap."

> " **Ramprakash, two days away from his 19th birthday, took them to within three runs of victory, batting throughout in his cap with confidence, style and a rare charm**

He continues: "I was very close to being lbw first ball to Graham Dilley. I might just have got outside the line! But Dickie Bird was on my Christmas card list after that. I managed to get into the game and block everything else out. I had a bit of a mix-up with Roland Butcher and he was run out. It was difficult but I

had to keep calm and try to create a partnership with another player. And luckily Embers was that player. He was a good guy to have in those situations." Emburey adds: "We were in trouble at 64 for 5. Ramps just played. He took it in his stride."

Wisden reported: "Ramprakash, two days away from his 19th birthday, took them to within three runs of victory, batting throughout in his cap with confidence, style and a rare charm." Ramprakash had made 56 when he was caught on the boundary. "I did feel good about getting fifty and I might have wanted to play a few shots to get it over with. But we were pretty much home. Everyone was happy when I came into the dressing room – even Roland.

"When you're 18 you don't realise how lucky you are to play in a trophy-winning side. I had a lot of top international players around me and I could see how happy they were. But I'd just come on the scene and it wasn't until later in my career when Middlesex had some tougher times that I really appreciated days like that."

Ramprakash received the man-of-the-match award from Geoff Boycott: "He was very generous in his praise but I think he might also have lambasted me for getting out." ●

At Lord's, September 3, 1988. Worcestershire 161-9 (60 overs) (PA Neale 64; SP Hughes 4-30); †Middlesex 162-7 (55.3 overs) (MR Ramprakash 56; GR Dilley 5-29). Man of the match: MR Ramprakash.

MARK RAVIN RAMPRAKASH
Born: September 5, 1969, Bushey
Right-hand batsman

- 2,350 runs at 27.32 in 52 Tests
- 15,046 first-class runs for Middlesex (35,659 overall, 114 hundreds) at 50.48 1987–2000
- Joint seventh-most first-class centuries (46) for Middlesex
- Has scored a century in each innings of a match for Middlesex four times – the county record
- 7,445 one-day runs (13,273 overall) for Middlesex
- Championship titles 1990, 1993
- One-day title 1988 (MoM)
- Middlesex cap 1990
- Middlesex captain 1997–99
- Middlesex benefit 2000
- Played for Surrey 2001–12

FIFTY NOT OUT

Chris Goldie reports on half a century of good work by the Middlesex Cricket Trust, raising funds and promoting the game throughout the county

In 1950, Middlesex CCC formed a Junior Cricket Committee aimed at "fostering the welfare of young cricketers". This committee oversaw the development of a temporary indoor school at Alexandra Palace ahead of the opening, in 1956, of the Middlesex County Cricket School at Finchley.

By 1964, the school had welcomed over 5,000 boys and organised outreach sessions to a number of the 955 state schools within the county boundaries. This pioneering work came at a cost and by 1963, the county club had spent over £9,000 on the delivery of this activity as well as £32,000 on the creation of the indoor school. Therefore the club resolved to form a charitable trust through which it could launch an appeal to raise £60,000 to ensure that this work could continue and expand without becoming a financial burden on Middlesex's limited resources.

The Middlesex County Cricket Club Centenary Youth Trust was born and the first to be established by any major cricket organisation in the country. The prime minister of the day, Sir Alec Douglas-Home, was one of a distinguished group of founding trustees and George Newman, then president of the county club, became chairman. In 2011, it was renamed the Middlesex Cricket Trust.

The trust has mostly been reactive, supporting requests for funding from clubs, schools and associations. At times it has been innovative. When it became compulsory for young people to wear helmets, the trust funded a wholesale supply of helmets to clubs. At times it has sought the support of cricket-lovers with a series of appeals and occasionally it has benefited dramatically from bequests, most notably a reasonable proportion of the estate of Gubby Allen, who had been president of MCC when the trust was first established.

As the trust embarks on its second half-century, its work continues to recognise challenges that face the game across the county and is strongly committed to funding innovative solutions. Working closely with the Middlesex Cricket Board, the trust not only funds improvements to ground facilities at clubs and schools but also seeks to attract and distribute funding for projects that use cricket to change lives, provide opportunities and promote social cohesion across the capital.

In recent years, the trust has worked with the Metropolitan Police in the Borough of Harrow and is now, with the support of generous gifts from the Lovering Foundation and the Sir John Cass Foundation, funding the development of local coaches from some of London's most deprived boroughs who will work specifically with local youths, many from the Asian communities of East London, to develop the natural latent talent that exists in these areas.

> **"When it became compulsory for young people to wear helmets, the trust funded a wholesale supply of helmets to clubs**

The Trust also is the principal funder of the schools' competitions in the county, and has seen participation increase as a direct result of our support. The trust has also provided the core funding to enable the establishment of Borough Development Groups across Middlesex, a network which provide Cricket Middlesex with direct and regular access to local cricket leadership.

Just as in 1964, these activities carry a cost and the Middlesex Cricket Trust is there to provide support as and where we can. To do so, the Middlesex Cricket Trust needs your support, whether as a Friend of MCT, a sponsor of a new initiative or by helping to spread the word as an ambassador for cricket in Middlesex. Just as our forefathers did in 1964, the trustees once again appeal to all cricket lovers to back our work and help the MCT to make a difference. ●

For more information, visit: *www.middlesexcrickettrust.org.uk*
Chris Goldie, who played for Hampshire and Cambridge University, is chairman of the Middlesex Cricket Trust, a member of the Middlesex CCC executive board, secretary of the Middlesex Cricket Board and chairman of Richmond CC

BY JOHN STERN

WHEN HARRY MET HENDO

Middlesex's Twenty20 campaign began with low expectations and rumblings of discontent off the field. It finished with a thriller at the Rose Bowl and a film star in the dressing room

Having lost 20 and won only ten of 32 Twenty20 matches prior to the 2008 season, hopes of a decent tilt at the shortest form of the game were not exactly stratospheric. To make matters worse, a members' petition had been started, calling for a vote of no confidence in the committee. The season was, *Wisden* reported euphemistically, "a strange and eventful one for Middlesex, on and off the field".

Ed Smith began the season as captain but broke an ankle two matches into the Twenty20 campaign. He recalls: "I was reading one of the papers on the way to our first game at the Rose Bowl and it gave us no chance even to win the game against 'all-star'

Hampshire who had Kevin Pietersen playing for them. I thought we were a lot better than that."

But against this background of what Smith calls "uncertainty and turmoil", Middlesex had won three successive matches (two in the Championship and one in the 50-over competition) before the start of the Twenty20. Supporter Peter Moore says: "There was rebellion in the air and people were signing the petition but then we started to win so we thought we'd better stop."

Smith had been "messing about in the background", analysing data from the IPL and discussing strategies with coach Toby Radford and senior players like Ed Joyce and Shaun Udal. "We

" Harry Potter – Daniel Radcliffe – was running around in the dressing room. He wasn't happy because he was a Durham fan and I had smoked his guys

went down a route of picking five good bowlers including two spinners," says Smith. "The other thing we thought about was lots and lots of bowling changes." The outcome was a battle plan: "From Rose Bowl to Rose Bowl – how we're going to win the Twenty20". But there was a snag. "I was late getting to the game so I just threw these print-outs at people in the dressing room – there's no way it could have gone in."

Whether the information was absorbed or not, Middlesex kicked off with an emphatic win over Hampshire. Owais Shah top-scored and Udal picked up three wickets against his old county. The following day at Lord's they strolled past Essex with 19 balls to spare. Five wins on the bounce in all competitions. "Out of nowhere," says Smith, "we had momentum – and not just in the T20."

Middlesex just kept on winning. Australian left-armer Dirk Nannes took a hat-trick in the return match against Essex and South African all-rounder Tyron Henderson, aka 'the Blacksmith', bludgeoned 64 off 30 balls in the run-chase. Two more wins virtually secured a place in the quarter-finals before the campaign briefly hit the buffers with back-to-back defeats.

The home quarter-final against Lancashire had to be played at The Oval because of a clash with the Lord's Test and it provided a televised stage for the 20-year-old left-hander Dawid Malan, Roehampton-born but South African-raised, to display his prodigious talent against a side containing six internationals including Andrew Flintoff. From 21 for 4 Middlesex recovered to post 176 for 7 thanks, almost exclusively, to Malan's 103 off 54 balls.

Flintoff carried Lancashire's hopes after they too made a poor start but having scored 53 from 41 balls he hit a leg-side full toss straight to Malan at deep square leg. Henderson, whose ability to bowl at the 'death' was what had first attracted Middlesex to him in 2007, and Indian slow left-armer Murali Kartik turned the screw to see their side home by 12 runs.

And so back to the Rose Bowl, where the campaign had started, for Middlesex's first experience of Twenty20 finals day. As if that wasn't enough there was the carrot of a trip to Antigua and a chance to win Allen Stanford's millions plus the chance to qualify for the inaugural Twenty20 Champions League (which, as it turned out, was cancelled following the Mumbai terrorist attacks).

In the first semi-final they faced Durham, who won the toss and batted first. But they never built up any serious momentum and were restricted to 138 for 6. Tim Murtagh got rid of Aussie opener Michael Di Venuto with the third ball and the two spinners, Udal and Kartik, conceded only 36 from their eight overs.

Middlesex cantered home with 26 balls to spare, their whip well and truly cracked by Henderson whose 59 not out came from only 21 balls and contained seven sixes. "Twenty-one balls!" laughs Henderson as he remembers the day. He was especially severe on Steve Harmison who had been recalled to England's Test side that day. "My second ball was from him and I hit it straight back over his head for six. I knew the next one wasn't going to be anywhere my half of the wicket so I was standing back waiting. It was a 94 mile-an-hour bouncer and I hit that into the crowd over square leg!"

The sense of fun in Henderson's voice as he relives the experience is infectious. "My take on Twenty20 is we're there to entertain," he says. "My role wasn't to block and push ones. My role was to get on with it and whatever was going to happen was going to happen fast. I might not have been there very long but if I hung around for a few balls there were going to be some fireworks!"

Henderson's primary skill was his 'death' bowling and the "clobbering" – as the acting captain Joyce puts it – was a bonus. But he managed to exhibit both aspects of his game in the final against Kent, a nail-biter that displayed Twenty20 cricket in its very best light.

Having won the toss, Middlesex posted the highest total in any of the

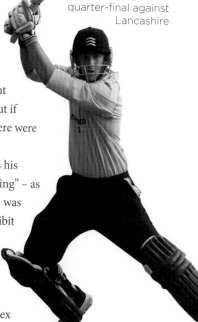

Full flow: Dawid Malan during his match-winning century in the quarter-final against Lancashire

six finals to date. The lynchpin was Shah whose 75 off 35 balls was described in *The Times*, perhaps understatedly, as "a touch of class". Three of his five sixes came from successive deliveries from off-spinner James Tredwell. Henderson weighed in with a relatively sedate 43 off 33 balls.

Kent's chase was a tall order but they just about managed to stay in touch. With South African Justin Kemp in full flight, they needed 16 from the final over. It was to be bowled by Henderson, who had borrowed kit from Kemp when he arrived to play for Kent in 2006 because his own gear had been lost in transit.

Kemp had already been given a life on 24 by Joyce. "Generally I fielded in the ring," Joyce remembers. "I must have changed the field and, because we were a bit slow on our overs, ran down to long off. I remember it very well. Murtagh was bowling. Usually you'd be clever with your positioning under the lights to make sure the lights aren't in your eye-line when the ball comes to you. But I hadn't done that. I saw the ball get hit, knew it was coming to me, knew it was catchable height but I literally didn't see it until the last minute. In the end I was glad it didn't just go straight through me for four. It actually hit near the middle of my hands which was a bit of a miracle.

"It was a hard moment because Kemp was batting so well at that stage. It was a bit of a heart-breaker at the time but you quickly forget about these things if you go on and win the game. It's probably easier being captain because there are so many other things to think about. Dropping catches is the worst thing in cricket – worse than getting nought. But it all added to the tension! It's a better way to win it than an easy victory because you get all the emotions."

Kemp scored two off the first ball of the last over and four, straight down the ground, off the second. The third ball looked to be a turning point. Malan's return from long-on was so wayward it went for two overthrows (four in total). Nerves were getting the better of Middlesex and Kent were now in sight of victory. The next ball was clubbed by Kemp towards Malan again. "Malan didn't even move," says Henderson. "Ed Joyce came round from cow corner to cut it off because he was too scared to move."

Kent needed only four from the last two balls but three would have been enough for them because they had lost fewer wickets. Henderson's 3.4 overs had gone for 58. The odds were heavily in favour of his fellow countryman and former team-mate Kemp. Was Henderson nervous? "It was do or die, it was a trip to Antigua, it was the Champions League – there wasn't much riding on it! But that's why you play the game, for situations like that. And it's what I practised for."

Doctor death: Tyron Henderson owned the end of the innings

> ## It was do or die, it was a trip to Antigua, it was the Champions League – there wasn't much riding on it!

The penultimate ball was full, just outside off stump and Kemp failed to make contact. Ben Scott, standing up to the stumps, took it and whipped off the bails. "I'll admit I took a chance with that ball," says Henderson, "because they needed four and I went for a slow yorker. Justin tried to run it down because I had third man up – and he missed it."

On Sky TV, David Lloyd squealed like a man receiving a full-body massage: "Ooo … ooo … ooo – what a game now! You could argue that's the best delivery of the game."

One ball left, still four to win. Whether Henderson was nervous or not, he was exhaling heavily at the start of his run-up. He produced the perfect yorker which Kemp succeeded only in hitting straight back to the bowler. "He got himself jammed up," says Henderson. Middlesex had won by three runs and secured their first trophy since the 1993 County Championship.

Cue mayhem. Pink-shirted Middlesex players amassed in a huddle like a giant strawberry ice cream. "The next thing I knew

I had Murali Kartik running at me from mid-wicket – I had to catch him because he took off from about six foot away," remembers Henderson. On Sky Nasser Hussain observed: "Look at these scenes – who needs the English Premier League when you've got this?"

"There was amazing euphoria," says Joyce. "I remember sprinting and just getting involved in a massive huddle. I can't remember anything about my speech but I do remember receiving the trophy and getting champagne sprayed all over me. We had a great time in the changing room afterwards. The Rose Bowl were really good with us and just let us stay in there. There were about ten members of my family who'd come over for the final and they were in the changing room along with 100 other miscellaneous people."

One of those miscellaneous people was something of a celebrity. "Harry Potter – Daniel Radcliffe – was running around in the dressing room," says Henderson. "He wasn't happy because he was a Durham fan and I had smoked his guys when I was batting.

"I had to do a drugs test so I got waylaid but after that the champagne flowed. My wife had flown over from South Africa for finals day and we went to bed about half past four in the morning. Eoin Morgan and Billy Godleman were still walking around in their cricket kit. Ben Scott and Joe Denly were sitting at – and playing – a piano, naked. Sky Sports wanted live pictures of me carrying the trophy out of the hotel the following morning and I couldn't find any of my guys to help. So in the end I got a mate of mine, who had flown over from Hong Kong for finals day, to help me carry the trophy out of the hotel – live on Sky Sports."

Henderson's adventure wasn't quite complete. He received a phone call telling him that he failed his drugs test. He was "strung along for about 15 minutes" until he spotted a prankster – Middlesex's irrepressible former wicketkeeper David Nash.

For Middlesex this unexpected trophy marked a corner turned, not to mention a trip to Antigua. For Henderson it yielded him an IPL contract with the Rajasthan Royals. He says: "Manoj Badali [the owner] is based in London and he had been watching the final. They gave me a stupid contract – $650,000. Unfortunately I didn't get to play much in the IPL but it was a very different experience. I can't say I regret any of it. I got to do what I wanted to do and people paid me money to do it – what more could you want?" ●

SOUTH DIVISION TABLE

	Mat	Won	Lost	Tied	N/R	Pts	Net RR
Middlesex	10	8	2	0	0	16	+0.732
Essex	10	6	3	1	0	13	+0.937
Kent	10	6	4	0	0	12	+0.640
Hampshire	10	5	4	1	0	11	-0.505
Sussex	10	2	8	0	0	4	-0.876
Surrey	10	2	8	0	0	4	-0.905

Quarter-final, July 8, The Oval. Middlesex beat Lancashire by 12 runs.
Middlesex 176-7 (20 overs) (DJ Malan 103 *off 54 balls*, EJG Morgan 33; A Flintoff 3-17); Lancashire 164-8 (20 overs) (Flintoff 53; TJ Murtagh 3-35).

Semi-final, July 26, Rose Bowl. Middlesex beat Durham by 8 wickets.
Durham 138-6 (20 overs) (S Chanderpaul 48, PD Collingwood 35; TJ Murtagh 3-29); Middlesex 141-2 (15.4 overs) (T Henderson 59* *off 21 balls with 7 sixes*, EC Joyce 41).

TWENTY 20 CUP FINAL, ROSE BOWL, JULY 26, 2008
KENT v MIDDLESEX
Toss: Middlesex. Result: Middlesex won by 3 runs. Man of the match: OA Shah.

MIDDLESEX		Runs	Balls
BA Godleman	b Yasir Arafat	1	6
*EC Joyce	c Jones b Cook	23	12
T Henderson	c Key b McLaren	43	33
OA Shah	b McLaren	75	35
EJG Morgan	c Tredwell b Azhar Mahmood	23	18
D J Malan	not out	6	8
S D Udal	b Yasir Arafat	1	3
†BJM Scott	not out	6	5
TJ Murtagh	did not bat		
M Kartik	did not bat		
DP Nannes	did not bat		
Extras	(5 b, 1 lb, 3 w)	9	
Total	**(6 wickets, 20 overs)**	**187**	

Fall of wickets: 1-19, 2-47, 3-83, 4-162, 5-173, 6-179

KENT	O	M	R	W
Yasir Arafat	4	0	20	2
Azhar Mahmood	4	0	33	1
McLaren	4	0	36	2
Cook	4	0	35	1
Tredwell	2	0	27	0
Stevens	2	0	30	0

KENT		Runs	Balls
JL Denly	c Godleman b Udal	31	25
*RWT Key	c Scott b Kartik	52	30
JM Kemp	run out (Henderson)	49	38
Yasir Arafat	run out (Joyce)	1	1
DI Stevens	c Joyce b Nannes	33	23
Azhar Mahmood	not out	6	4
M van Jaarsveld	did not bat		
R McLaren	did not bat		
†GO Jones	did not bat		
JC Tredwell	did not bat		
SJ Cook	did not bat		
Extras	(6 lb, 2 nb, 4 w)	12	
Total	**(5 wickets, 20 overs)**	**184**	

Fall of wickets: 1-89, 2-91, 3-96, 4-166, 5-184

KENT	O	M	R	W
Murtagh	4	0	32	0
Nannes	4	0	37	1
Henderson	4	0	58	0
Kartik	4	0	30	1
Udal	4	0	21	1

Umpires: JW Lloyds, NA Mallender

VIEW FROM THE
COMMENTARY BOX

BBC London's **Kevin Hand** on life on the road following the Seaxes and discovering the global following for county cricket

There are times when my job gets a bit surreal: there I am, sitting in the *Test Match Special* box at Lord's when someone emails in from Antarctica and starts a discussion on chinstrap penguins.

Yes, that really did happen. A research team down at the bottom of the world had logged on to the BBC London website to hear commentary on a Middlesex Championship fixture and naturally our other listeners wanted to know what they were doing there.

The enthusiastic following our commentaries receive is just one sign of the recent resurgence of county cricket, demonstrating that while attendances at Championship games remain small, the interest away from the grounds is huge, and by no means restricted to the UK.

In 2003, BBC London 94.9 were online pioneers with ball-by-ball coverage of Surrey's season and the following year the service was extended to Middlesex; ten years later and every county game is covered online, with a featured match on Five Live Sports Extra most weeks, and

even medium-wave coverage in some parts of the country.

Middlesex's followers, from every corner of the world, have played their part in the success of the show with interactions via Twitter and email. The service would be far less entertaining without those sometimes knowledgeable and often humorous contributions.

The ball-by-ball coverage is not a first, though; in the 1970s BBC Radio London, as it was then known, was among the first of the local stations to cover the John Player League, as well as offering extended reports from the Championship.

Sadly the man who became a legend in those early days, Norman de Mesquita, passed away in 2013 but he left behind a great legacy. The messages and memories that were shared by those that remembered fondly his broadcasts on Sunday afternoons were overwhelming after his sudden death in July, at the age of 81.

Having started his working life as

Sound of summer: Kevin at sunny Taunton

Sidekick: David 'DT' Townsend

an actor, Norman enjoyed a long and illustrious career as a reporter and commentator on his two great loves, cricket and ice hockey. He also recalled with relish trips across Europe reporting on London's football teams.

Norman's voice and delivery were compared to John Arlott's and he was a member of the *Test Match Special*

Perk of the job: Kevin presents 2008 Twenty20 Cup-winning captain Ed Joyce with a BBC London Team of the Year award

" Listeners tune in from anywhere in the world for familiar sounds of home or, as has been the case in America, an introduction to the sport

team that covered the 1979 World Cup in England.

Sadly, illness in his latter years, which severely affected his speech, denied me the opportunity to invite him on air and have the chance to share the mic with a man who will be remembered as one of the greats of county cricket commentary from its formative years.

He remained an ever-present at Lord's, though, as he continued to report for *Wisden*, and his presence, and humour, is already greatly missed. In recent seasons, I know it pleased Norman greatly to see the county that he supported as a boy growing up in Edgware, restored to the verge of former glories.

It has been my privilege to witness that transformation, too, from the dark days of Division Two, to genuine title contenders

under the guidance of Gus Fraser.

The current BBC service has a commentator for each county travelling home and away to double up, along with guests, to provide the coverage. Among those guests is another Middlesex commentator from yesteryear, David Townsend, who covered the county for CricketCall from 1988–90. DT has now returned to summarise for Middlesex since retiring from the media, perhaps sensing that a helping hand would be more than appreciated and never slow to remind me that in his day there were three broadcasters at each game, not just one, as it was for several seasons, or two, as it is now.

The advantage of the current internet incarnation of the broadcast is the listeners' ability to tune in anywhere in

the world, whether to hear the familiar sounds of home or, as has been the case in particular for a number of regulars in America, an introduction to the sport.

The BBC's commitment in 2013 to covering all 18 counties in every competition is, hopefully, an indication that the commentaries will last the test of time. There is clearly an appetite for county coverage and with the increased use of digital platforms for broadcasting, hopefully, there won't be any more gaps in coverage of the summer game, or any more seasons when one cannot log on to hear a man sitting in a box at Lord's talking about cricket and chinstrap penguins. ●

For more information on Kevin's online coverage of Middlesex visit www.bbc.co.uk/cricket

INTERVIEW BY JOHN STERN

KEEPING THE FAITH

Join the debate: (left to right) Keith Roberts, Roy Simmons and Peter Moore

Three of Middlesex's most ardent supporters, all contributors to the Middlesex Till We Die website, give their views on the club and what the county means to them

When did you first start following Middlesex?

Keith Roberts: Only about 16 years ago. I've always loved the sport and a friend took me along to a one-day game against Lancashire. I was hooked. I started going on my own, didn't know anybody. Then I went out to the Stanford Series, met a guy called Kev through the website and we hit it off and then you meet other people. It's just a lovely journey. Everyone's so sociable. You don't get any supporter segregation.

Roy Simmons: I go back to the summer of '47. I followed them through school days. My dad was born in Islington and he was a proper Middlesex chap but he used to go on about Jack Hobbs. My first game was a benefit game for Denis Compton at Stanmore then my first-class debut was in 1961 and a young bloke called Mike Brearley was also making his debut at Lord's. He found the quicker bowlers a bit hot stuff.

How do you think the club is doing now?

Peter Moore: Ten or 12 years ago we were in a desperate state. I was a rebel and quite outspoken about the way the club was run. There was a great deal of unrest for a variety of reasons. We changed the committee structure and I made a promise that if I thought the club was heading in the right direction I would get behind that. And I think we are. Angus has done a tremendous job. He has such power and respect at the club that he was the only person who could bring Mark Ramprakash back to the club without any murmurs. People asked me what I thought and I said, "If it's good enough for Angus, it's good enough for me."

Roberts: This is our year. I said to Vinny [Codrington, chief executive] that when Fred Titmus died in 2011 we would win the second division for Fred. We did and I reckon we'll win Division One in our anniversary year.

Moore: It's very important what's happening at Radlett.

Simmons: We've now got a proper place to train and for pre-season.

Moore: I want to mention Vinny because we are at a disadvantage compared to Surrey who are made of money. It's probably hard for us to lose a lot of money but it's hard to make much money. Vinny does a tremendous job. He changed things. Chris Rogers was a tremendous signing. He's an old-fashioned player who commands respect.

> **" At away games opposition supporters greet you with open arms**

Who have been your favourite players?

Simmons: I absolutely loved Desmond Haynes.

Roberts: I'd agree with that.

Moore: He turned Mike Roseberry into a very decent player.

Roberts: I was watching some beach cricket in Antigua at the Stanford Series and one of the teams was captained by Desi. I called out to him at one stage and pointed to the badge on my Middlesex shirt and he grinned back and gave a big thumbs-up. It's clear that the club still means a lot to him.

Moore: Titmus played for us in five different decades and that will never

THE FANS

KEITH 'BEEFY' ROBERTS
Born: April 17, 1964
Lives: Uxbridge
Occupation: London
Underground maintenance

ROY SIMMONS
Born: January 16, 1938
Lives: Pinner
Occupation: Retired British
Airways finance systems
analyst

PETER MOORE
Born: November 12, 1952
Lives: Abbots Langley
Occupation: Retired solicitor

happen again. Our greatest servant. I saw him in the Lord's shop about five years before he passed away and no one recognised him. So I went up to him: "Mr Titmus, you are probably our greatest ever servant" and there were tears in his eyes.

Do you travel to away games?
Roberts: In 2012 I went a bit silly because it was the first season back in Division One. I did virtually every day of every Championship game and the 40-over games. A few of us, who are involved with Middlesex Till We Die, get together and sort out hotels and book train tickets a long way in advance. I can take or leave Twenty20. At away games opposition supporters greet you with open arms. At Trent Bridge last year I was sitting in the pavilion and this guy came over and asked if I was OK. "Yeah, why shouldn't I be?" Turned out he was the president. He said: "I just wanted to make sure that our visitors from Middlesex were being properly looked after."

You meet so many different people and lots of characters that you would only ever see at the cricket. It used to be that I would only see or be in touch with the guys I went to the cricket with during the season and then once it was over that would be it. But I decided that it shouldn't be like that, that we should be friends out of season too.

We went to Grace Road, Leicester, for the last game of the 2011 season and the people were so friendly. At the end of the second day we wanted to get into town so we asked one of the officials where the bus stop for the city centre was. He told us. Then while we were waiting for the bus, a car pulled up. It was the same guy. He said, "Don't bother with the bus – I'll give you a lift." It was the chief executive.

The players are also really appreciative and they're pleased to see you. They respect you do for doing it and it makes you want to do it more.

Do you care about England's fortunes as much as Middlesex's?
Simmons: I'm probably Middlesex first.
Roberts: Club first.
Moore: What annoyed me last year was when the powers that be thought it was a good idea to schedule Surrey against Middlesex at The Oval during the Lord's Test. Surely it could be arranged that Surrey and Middlesex are playing away when there are Test matches in London. The problem is that county cricket is at the bottom of the food chain.

What does Middlesex mean to you?
Roberts: It means a hell of a lot.
Moore: When I lived in Stanmore I always used to put Stanmore, Middlesex on the postcode.
Simmons: I've been volunteering for the club since 2008, helping to promote out-ground matches. I've have travelled from Fulham and Staines all the way up to Buckinghamshire. Everywhere you go the goodwill towards Middlesex is huge.
Moore: I find it disappointing that in the Lord's shop you have two Surrey cricketers –

Mark Butcher and Alec Stewart – advertising the clothing. We still have our identity and we're still one of the great counties.

Could you ever imagine Middlesex moving away from Lord's and having their own stand-alone identity elsewhere?
Simmons: I don't think that the financial deal at Lord's is that wonderful but one of the advantages of Lord's to us is T20.
Moore: There is a danger that if Middlesex left Lord's would we, in 20 years time, be any bigger than Leicester or Derby? ●

THE SEAXE CLUB

The Seaxe Club is Middlesex's official supporters' club and membership of the Seaxe Club is open to all members of Middlesex CCC. Seaxe supports cricket within the County of Middlesex and promotes the game at all levels within the County. The club supports youth cricket, the county side and holds social events throughout the year. For most Middlesex matches at Lord's Seaxe have exclusive use of a double box in the Tavern Stand. Here you can watch the cricket in comfort and have a cup of tea and home made cake, find out about social events and borrow books. The club holds winter socials, annual awards ceremonies, race nights and much more. For further information please visit www.seaxeclub.co.uk

SELECT SEAXES

With so many great players to choose from the task for our eminent and experienced panel to pick Middlesex's best post-war side was no easy one

THE JUDGES

Terry Cooper - Middlesex reporter for *Wisden* and the Press Association for more than 25 years and author of the Fred Titmus profile on pages 68-71.

John Murray - The great Middlesex and England wicketkeeper whose career spanned 25 years from 1952–75. He is interviewed on pages 62–67.

Roy Simmons - A follower of the club since the Compton-Edrich era and contributor to the Middlesex Till We Die website.

Rob Steen - journalist, author and supporter of Middlesex since the 1960s. Author of the profiles of Jack Robertson (pages 60-61) and Desmond Haynes (pages 82-83)

Marcus Williams - First watched Middlesex in 1956; worked for *The Times* sports desk for over 30 years and has contributed a number of the older historical articles in this brochure.

THE VERDICT

	MIDDLESEX RECORD (FIRST-CLASS)
1. Jack Robertson (1937–59)	27,088 runs at 38.36, 59 hundreds
2. Desmond Haynes (1989–94)	7,071 runs at 49.10, 21 hundreds
3. Bill Edrich (1937–58)	25,738 runs at 43.40, 62 hundreds; 328 wickets at 30.41
4. Denis Compton (1936–58)	21,781 runs at 49.95, 67 hundreds; 477 wickets at 29.61
5. Mike Gatting (1975–98)	28,411 runs at 52.80, 77 hundreds; 129 wickets at 28.29
6. Mike Brearley, capt (1961–83)	15,985 runs at 38.33, 29 hundreds
7. John Murray, wk (1952–75)	15,251 runs at 23.24, 11 hundreds; 1,024 catches, 200 stumping
8. Fred Titmus (1949–82)	17,320 runs at 22.78, 5 hundreds; 2,361 wickets at 21.27
9. Phil Edmonds (1971–92)	5,036 runs at 19.82; 883 wickets at 23.55
10. Angus Fraser (1984–2002)	2,431 runs at 12.34; 679 wickets at 26.41
11. Wayne Daniel (1977–88)	1,043 runs at 10.32; 685 wickets at 22.02

12TH MAN (RESERVE SEAMER)

Alan Moss (1950–63)	1,234 runs at 6.52; 1,088 wickets at 19.81
John Price (1961–75)	902 runs at 8.12; 734 wickets 22.39

12TH MAN (SUBSTITUTE FIELDER)

Peter Parfitt (1956–72)	21,302 runs at 36.66; 453 catches

THE CRITERIA

To select an XI to play a first-class match; two overseas players allowed; selection should be based solely on performances for Middlesex, rather than for England or other representative teams.

There were only three unanimous choices – Mike Gatting, Denis Compton and Fred Titmus – but given that John Murray was a selector and disinclined to pick himself, he too can, quite rightly, be included in that elite group. Jack Robertson, Desmond Haynes, Bill Edrich and Wayne Daniel all picked up four votes each. "Desi was the finest opener I have seen playing for Middlesex, adept at all forms of the game," said Roy Simmons while John Murray talks of Haynes's five seasons with the county as "a proper career".

The marginal selection, based on the conditions in our notional contest, is between Phil Edmonds and an extra seam bowler. Alan Moss and John Price , who carried the bowling attack for much of his

15-year career, both picked up two votes each. Back-up seam bowling comes from Edrich and Gatting ("in his younger guise," said Marcus Williams). And we mustn't forget Compo's chinamen for an additional spin option.

In the leadership election Brearley secured a majority – just – to skipper this highly-talented, and strong-minded team. "With so much mercurial talent a strong captain is essential and there is nobody better to get the best out of them than Brearley," said Marcus. There was a vote each for Gubby Allen and Gatting as captain. "Gatt might wish he stayed as MCC president," reckoned Terry Cooper. "He's only in charge of 18,000 blokes there. Now he's got Ramps, Fred and Edmonds." Terry had Mark Ramprakash in his line-up.

The over-riding sentiment among the panel was regret at having to leave so many good players out. Rob Steen apologised, in particular, to: "Messrs Murtagh, Radley, Selvey and Emburey." Marcus gave honourable mentions also to Peter Parfitt, Norman Cowans and Vince van der Bijl.

The selections for 12th man varied from reserve bowlers to electric sub fielders, for which spot Parfitt won out over Roland Butcher and Graham Barlow.

MIDDLESEX'S GREATEST PRE-WAR XI

The first 75 years of Middlesex's history are strewn with outstanding players and although the selector of this pre-war XI is too young to have seen any of them in action, he is confident that they could give their post-war counterparts a very good run for their money.

This side has immense depth in batting – MacGregor, the wicketkeeper, at no. 9 scored three first-class hundreds – and five genuine all-rounders not to mention that all bar one, but including the 12th man, won Test caps. The odd man out was Tarrant but his career figures mark him out as an exceptional talent and it was his move to England that almost certainly cost him the chance of a place in the Australian side.

With JT Hearne, Allen, Trott and Haig to do the faster bowling and Peebles, Tarrant and JW Hearne to provide the spin there is plenty of variety in the attack. Durston might swap places with Peebles if there's a bit of green in the pitch.

Warner (right), on the strength of many years at the Middlesex helm and notably the great 1920 Championship triumph, earns the captaincy, although Stoddart – like Warner – did lead a victorious Ashes campaign in Australia. **Marcus Williams**

MIDDLESEX RECORD (FIRST-CLASS)

	MIDDLESEX RECORD (FIRST-CLASS)
1. Pelham Warner, capt (1894–1920)	19,507 runs at 37.44, 46 hundreds
2. Frank Tarrant (1904–14)	12,169 runs at 38.02, 26 hundreds; 1,005 wickets at 17.43
3. JW Hearne (1909–36)	27,612 runs at 41.15, 71 hundreds; 1,438 wickets at 23.16
4. Patsy Hendren (1907–37)	40,302 runs at 49.81, 119 hundreds
5. Andrew Stoddart (1885–1900)	9,255 runs at 31.80, 16 hundreds; 141 wickets at 28.63
6. Nigel Haig (1912–34)	12,289 runs at 20.79, 11 hundreds; 931 wickets at 26.06
7. Gubby Allen (1921–50)	4,668 runs at 25.64, 4 hundreds; 420 wickets at 20.63
8. Albert Trott (1898–1910)	6,253 runs at 20.23, 6 hundreds; 946 wickets at 21.49
9. Gregor MacGregor (wk, 1892–1907)	4,846 runs at 19.61, 2 hundreds; 279 catches, 111 stumpings
10. Ian Peebles (1928–48)	1,363 runs at 9.02; 610 wickets at 19.87
11. JT Hearne (1888–1923)	4,598 runs at 11.29; 2,093 wickets at 18.23
12th man: Jack Durston (1919–33)	3,569 runs at 11.62; 1,178 wickets at 21.96

BY MARCUS WILLIAMS

WALKING THE WALK FOR
150 YEARS

1864 Middlesex CCC founded at London Tavern, Bishopsgate Street, on February 2. First home match, at Cattle Market ground, Islington in June, brings victory by innings and 52 runs over Sussex. VE (Teddy) Walker, captain, takes 14 for 103. All out 20 v MCC, still county's lowest score.

1865 Teddy Walker claims 10 for 104 in Lancashire's second innings at Old Trafford. Charles Buller scores first century for Middlesex in inter-county match, 105* v Surrey at The Oval.

1866 Win six matches out of eight and are judged "champion county", being invited by MCC to play rest of England at Lord's in following season. Lose by an innings and 25 runs but have worse of conditions.

1869 Leave Islington and play home encounter of season with only two matches at Lord's, defeating Surrey by 43 runs.

1871 First (and last) match at Lillie Bridge ground, West Brompton, drawn against Surrey.

1872 Move to Prince's ground, Knightsbridge, and lose opener to Yorkshire by two wickets.

1876 Nottinghamshire match at Prince's abandoned when groundsman and former top wicketkeeper Tom Box drops dead working on scoreboard. Surrey match at The Oval tied for second time in eight years.

1877 After many overtures from MCC Middlesex finally move to Lord's but lose all four matches played there.

1878 With three wins, three draws and no defeats Middlesex have claims to be "champion county".

1885 All out 25 v Surrey at The Oval, county's lowest Championship total.

1886 A week after scoring 485 for Hampstead against the Stoics AE Stoddart scores his first century for Middlesex against Kent at Gravesend.

1887 Fresh from 192* against Kent, captain AJ Webbe scores 243* at Huddersfield, first double century for Middlesex in a county match and still their best against Yorkshire.

1888 George Burton takes all ten Surrey first-innings wickets for 59 at The Oval, and 13 in match, and follows up with 16 wickets in next match against Yorkshire at Sheffield. Was later county scorer.

1890 JT Hearne takes 6 for 62 on Championship debut against

ROLL OF HONOUR

County Championship Titles
1903, 1920, 1921, 1947 , 1949 *(shared)*,
1976, 1977 *(shared)*, 1980, 1982, 1985,
1990, 1993, *2011 Div Two winners*

One-Day Trophies
1977 Gillette Cup, **1980** Gillette Cup,
1983 Benson & Hedges Cup, **1984** NatWes
Trophy, **1986** Benson & Hedges Cup,
1988 NatWest Trophy, *2004 totesport
League Div 2 winners*, **2008** Twenty20 Cu

Nottinghamshire at Lord's. In following season he has 118 wickets in 16 county matches (avge 10.39) and takes 100 wickets or more for county in each season up to 1898.

1893 Stoddart becomes first Middlesex batsman to score two hundreds in match – 195* and 124 v Nottinghamshire at Lord's – and first to score 1,000 runs in season (1,178, avge 47.12). A weakened Middlesex side loses to Australians by 390 runs.

1897 Middlesex do not record a Championship win until August 14, against Sussex. County cap is introduced: dark blue with three seaxes.

1898 Middlesex win ten of final 12 matches, last seven in a row, to finish runners-up behind Yorkshire. Albert Trott (above) takes 102 wickets in first season for county despite missing several matches because of a hand injury. Webbe gives up captaincy after 14 seasons.

1899 Middlesex again runners-up, this time to Surrey. In opening sequence of six successive wins Middlesex (86) beat Somerset (35 and 44) by an innings and seven runs at Lord's, Hearne and Trott bowling them out twice in a total of 31.3 overs. Match lasts 3hr 5min, shortest completed first-class match. Against Kent at Lord's Richard Nicholls and 'Micky' Roche put on 230 for tenth wicket, then a world record and still county's best, after first nine wickets fall for 55. Another heavy defeat by Australians – innings and 230 runs – although Trott, playing against them for MCC, achieves unique feat of hitting ball over current Lord's pavilion.

1900 Stoddart scores 221 against Somerset at Lord's on final Middlesex appearance in JT Hearne's benefit match. In return match at Taunton Trott takes 10-42 in first innings.

1902 Middlesex earn cosmopolitan tag: Beldam (French descent), Ahsan-ul-Hak (from area now Pakistan), Robertson (born Peru), Dalmeny (Scottish), Bosanquet (Huguenot), Schwarz (father from Silesia), Warner (born Trinidad), Rawlin (born Yorkshire), Hearne (born Buckinghamshire).

1903 Middlesex champions, winning eight of 16 matches. Warner leads team in early part of season while official captain Gregor MacGregor is unavailable. Title secured with innings and 94-run win at The Oval. Warner goes on to lead England to 3-2 Ashes victory in Australia.

1904 Tie with South Africans, first such finish in major match at Lord's since 1839.

1905 Bernard Bosanquet, inventor of googly, scores hundred in each innings and takes 11 wickets in 374-run win over Sussex at Lord's.

1907 Trott takes four wickets in four balls and hat-trick in same innings of own benefit match against Somerset. Frank Tarrant becomes first Middlesex player to achieve double with 1,077 runs and 123 wickets. Match at Lord's abandoned by Lancashire captain Archie MacLaren, claiming pitch damaged by spectators angry that play on second day called off after rain.

1914 Middlesex runners-up. Tarrant breaks county record with 250* against Essex at Leyton and scores 200 in next match against Worcestershire, as well as 198 v Lancashire. JW Hearne makes eight hundreds, best 204 v Lancashire when he and Tarrant put on 380 for second wicket, and passes 2,000 runs for season. Both again achieve double. Trott commits suicide.

1920 Middlesex champions (above) after winning last nine games. Title clinched in memorable 55-run win over Surrey at Lord's, Plum Warner's final game for county. More than 52,000 pay for admission. In May bank holiday match first-class record set as top four batsmen (Warner, Lee, Hearne and Haig) score hundreds in total of 543 for 4 dec v Sussex. Championship celebrated with banquet at Café Royal. County makes profit of £3,270, of which £1,100 goes to MCC.

1921 Champions again – and again secured by victory over Surrey in final match at Lord's by six wickets under captaincy of Frank Mann.

1922 Russy Walker dies, ending family's unbroken connection with club.

1923 Hendren (above) scores 2,593 runs (avge 83.64) for county including 11 centuries. One of those is against Hampshire when Middlesex score 642-3 dec against Hampshire, still the county's record. Top four (Dales, Lee and JW Hearne are the others) again make hundreds.

1924 Runners-up to Yorkshire. Gloucestershire dismissed for 31 – the lowest total against Middlesex – (Haig 6-11, Durston 4-18) at Bristol but recover to win by 61 runs.

1925 Middlesex score 502 - 6 to beat Nottinghamshire at Trent Bridge despite losing first four wickets for 66. Still a Championship fourth-innings record.

1929 Top five places in bowling averages filled by amateurs, of whom Ian

Peebles, Walter Robins and Nigel Haig pass 100 wickets. Gubby Allen takes 10-40 v Lancashire at Lord's, still county's best analysis. JW Hearne breaks county record with 285* against Essex at Leyton.

1933 Hendren scores Middlesex's first triple hundred, 301* v Worcestershire at Dudley.

1935 Gubby Allen (above) tops national bowling averages. Middlesex II win Minor Counties Championship.

1936 Runners-up. JW Hearne plays final match, aged 45; Denis Compton plays first, aged 18.

1937 Runners-up again. Hendren, aged 48, retires with a flourish: five centuries in last 13 innings and career totals of 40,302 runs and 119 centuries for Middlesex. Bill Edrich scores 1,600 runs in debut season.

1938 Runners-up to Yorkshire for third season. Edrich completes 1,000 runs in all matches before end of May.

1939 Runners-up to Yorkshire for fourth time. Middlesex play 'home' match at The Oval when Lord's is unavailable because of Eton v Harrow match.

1946 Cricket resumes after Second World War and Middlesex are runners-up to Yorkshire for fifth time. Middlesex suffer heaviest defeat at Lord's: innings and 263 runs against Indians.

1947 Champions at last in Compton and Edrich's *annus mirabilis* (above) under inspiring captaincy of Walter Robins. Nineteen wins out of 26, including seven out of nine when dynamic duo are away at Tests. Compton's 3,816 runs and 18 centuries in all matches are record-breakers; Edrich's 3,539 stands second. Jack Robertson and Syd Brown also pass 2,000. Crowds flock to Lord's, nearly 30,000 present on Whit Monday.

1948 Compton and Edrich put on 424 for third wicket against Somerset at Lord's, still highest partnership for county.

1949 Joint champions with Yorkshire. Five players (Mann, Edrich, Compton, Young and Robertson) chosen for second Test v New Zealand. Robertson sets county record with 331* at Worcester in first-day total of 623-5 dec. Fred Titmus makes debut, aged 16, against Somerset at Bath.

1955 Titmus sets county record of 158 wickets, beating Trott's 154 in 1900. He also completes double, first Middlesex player since Robins and Haig in 1929.

1957 Compton makes 143 and 48 against Worcestershire at Lord's on final appearance as professional for Middlesex. John Murray (batting above) completes wicketkeeper's double of 1,000 runs and 100 dismissals in all matches, only previously achieved by Les Ames.

1961 Ian Bedford, aged 31, appointed captain after 11-year absence from county cricket.

1967 First Championship match at Lord's with Sunday play marred by slow Middlesex batting (371-7 off 176 overs) against Hampshire, which draws wide condemnation. By contrast return match at Portsmouth ends in tie.

1968 Titmus loses four toes in boating accident during England tour of

West Indies but tops county batting averages and takes 100 wickets.

1971 Brearley takes over captaincy. Middlesex lead table mid-season but finish sixth. Titmus takes 100 wickets in all matches for 16th time.

1972 Middlesex dismissed for 41 by Essex in Gillette Cup on "under-prepared" pitch at Westcliff, lowest total by first-class county in competition. Win inaugural Under-25 county competition.

1973 Titmus (above) becomes leading wicket-taker, passing JT Hearne's total of 2,133, and joins WG Grace, George Hirst and Wilfred Rhodes with 20,000 runs and 2,500 wickets. Under-25 competition retained.

1974 Win Under-25 competition for third time and are Second XI champions. Dismissed for 23 by Yorkshire in John Player League, still lowest total in English one-day cricket.

1975 Reach two cup finals but lose to Leicestershire in B&H and Lancashire in Gillette. They also lose in Under-25 final. Murray marks last season by beating Herbert Strudwick's wicketkeeping record of 1,495 dismissals.

1976 County champions. Title secured at The Oval, watched by three members of 1949 side (Edrich, Mann and Harry Sharp). Part-time off-spinner Norman Featherstone tops national bowling averages. Beat West Indians by four wickets.

1977 Championship shared with Kent. Gillette Cup won for first time with five-wicket win over Glamorgan. Rearranged home match against Somerset played at Chelmsford. Brearley leads England to 3-0 home Ashes win.

1980 County champions (above at Buckingham Palace)and Gillette Cup winners with seven-wicket win over Surrey. First Championship match at Uxbridge (v Derbyshire).

1981 Middlesex become first county to field full XI of Test players in Championship: Brearley, Downton,

Radley, Gatting, Butcher, Barlow, Emburey, Edmonds, Selvey, Thomson, Daniel. Team finishes fourth.

1982 Middlesex champions in Brearley's final season. Title is clinched at Worcester and Brearley makes winning hit in ten-wicket victory.

1983 B&H Cup winners against Essex and runners-up to same county Essex in Championship as Gatting (below) takes over captaincy.

1984 Beat Kent by four wickets to win NatWest Trophy. Gatting first to score 2,000 runs in a season for Middlesex – including 258 v Somerset at Bath – since Eric Russell in 1964.

1985 Another Championship despite Gatting, Downton, Edmonds, Emburey and Cowans missing many matches because of international calls.

1986 B&H Cup won with two-wicket win over Kent.

1987 Win only two Championship games and finish one from bottom. Mark Ramprakash, aged 17, scores 63* on debut v Yorkshire.

1988 NatWest Trophy winners, beating Worcestershire by three wickets.

1989 Lose by four wickets to Warwickshire in NatWest Trophy final. Second XI win championship and Bain Clarkson (55-over) Trophy.

1990 Champions. Top five batsmen (Haynes, Roseberry, Gatting, Ramprakash, Brown) play in all 22 matches. Also win Refuge Assurance Cup (contested by top four in Sunday league).

1991 No Championship win until August 12 and worst decline by reigning champions (14 places). First Sunday league game away from Lord's played at Southgate.

1992 Middlesex win Sunday league for first time, starting campaign with 12 successive wins.

1993 Championship secured by run of nine wins and two draws in 11 matches. Only defeat, by an innings in two days, comes in final match at Worcester.

1994 Richard Johnson, aged 19, takes 10-45 v Derbyshire at Derby, second youngest to achieve feat. John Carr tops national batting averages, 1,543 runs (avge 90.76), including 261* v Gloucestershire at Lord's.

1995 Runners-up. Ramprakash tops national averages with 2,258 runs (avge 77.86) including sequence of nine centuries in 14 Championship innings.

1996 Gatting completes set of first-class centuries against each county with 171 v Durham.

1997 Captain since 1983, Gatting hands over mid-season to Ramprakash (above); both score hundreds in next match. Don Bennett, player from 1950 to 1968, retires after 29 years as coach. Middlesex lose to Ireland in B&H Cup.

1998 Middlesex finish 17th out of 18, losing nine matches including last five (worst run since 1933). Gatting retires as player after 24 seasons and becomes director of coaching, replacing John Buchanan.

1999 Finish16th, bringing place in Championship second division for next season. Also lose to Cambridge University. Ramprakash resigns captaincy.

2000 Gatting (director of coaching), Ian Gould (coach) and Ramprakash all depart. First match at Richmond.

2001 Beat Australians for first time in 33 attempts, by six wickets in 50-over game – but lose to Herefordshire in C&G Trophy.

2002 Angus Fraser retires after six matches to become *Independent* cricket correspondent; Andrew Strauss takes over captaincy. Win promotion to Championship first division.

2003 Phil Tufnell quits two days before start of season to take up TV career. Concede 734-5 dec to Lancashire and follow on despite making highest ever total (544) by team forced to do so.

2004 Win totesport League second division. Season of four captains (Strauss, Shah, Joyce, Hutton) and five overseas players (Hayward, Klusener, Agarkar, McGrath, Clark).

2006 Bottom and relegated in both Championship and 40-over league. No Championship wins at Lord's, matching 1902, 1987 and 2000.

2007 Promoted from Pro40 League, winning play-off against Northamptonshire. New coach Richard Pybus leaves three months into three-year contract. Concede 850-7 dec against Somerset (including 315 by former captain Justin Langer), record total against them.

2008 Twenty20 Cup winners (above), beating Kent by three runs in final at Southampton, but relegated in Pro40 League. Fraser returns as managing director of cricket.

2010 Season begins with four successive Championship defeats, worst opening since 1885, and second successive one-from-bottom finish.

2011 Second division champions, led by Neil Dexter. Bottom in T20 south group, conceding 254-3 to Gloucestershire at Uxbridge including an unprecedented two centuries.

2012 Third in first division; runners-up in CB40 group but miss out on semi-finals. First-class match v Durham University played at Merchant Taylors' School.

2013 Ramprakash returns as part-time batting coach. Chris Rogers called up by Australia for Ashes at age of 35. YB40 match v Yorkshire played at Radlett. Toby Roland-Jones takes first Middlesex hat-trick since Phil Edmonds in 1981. Tim Murtagh is leading wicket-taker for fifth time in seven seasons since joining club from Surrey. ●

MIDDLESEX CCC
150TH ANNIVERSARY EVENTS

FEBRUARY 2ND

Commemorative Church Service at St John's Wood Church followed by champagne reception in the Long Room

MARCH 28TH

Launch lunch in the Nursery Pavilion with chairman of England selectors Geoff Miller and Middlesex greats

JUNE/JULY (TBC)

MCC President's XI vs Middlesex President's XI – Twenty 20 match at Lord's

JULY (TBC)

Middlesex XI vs Royal Household XI at Windsor Great Park

SEPTEMBER 30TH

Anniversary Gala Dinner (black tie) at the Honourable Artillery Company

DECEMBER (TBC)

Carol Concert in the Long Room at Lord's.

In addition there is the Annual Golf Day and and the Annual Corporate Seven-a-side cricket tournament at Wormsley (dates tbc)

Dates of some of the events were yet to be confirmed at the time of publication. Please visit **www.middlesexccc.com** for further details.